# Oneskein

# Oneskein

## 30 QUICK PROJECTS TO KNIT AND CROCHET

*photography by John Mulligan*

INTERWEAVE
interweavebooks.com

**Design** Leigh Radford
**Photo styling** Leigh Radford
**Illustrations** Gayle Ford
**Photography** John Mulligan

Interweave Press LLC
201 East Fourth Street
Loveland, CO 80537-5655 USA
interweavebooks.com


Printed and bound in China by Pimlico Book International.

Library of Congress Cataloging-in-Publication Data

Radford, Leigh.
One-skein knitting: 30 quick projects to knit and crochet
Leigh Radford.
        p. cm.
Includes bibliographical references and index.
ISBN 978-1-931499-74-3 (alk. paper)
1.  Knitting—Patterns. 2.  Crocheting—Patterns.  I. Title.
 TT825.R286 2006
 746.43'2—dc22

2005022358


15  14  13  12  11  10  9

*for my brother, Matt*

# contents

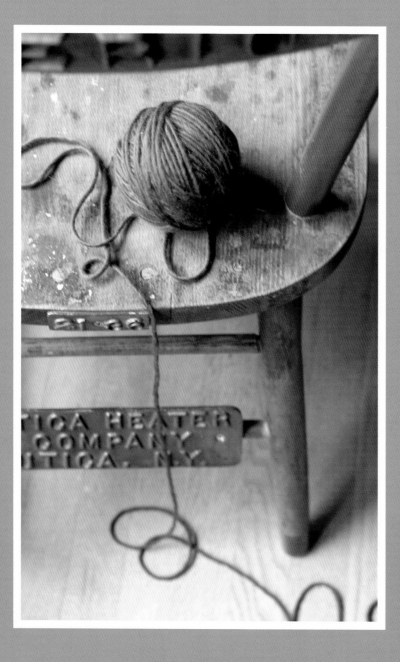

# introduction

The creative possibilities found in just one skein of yarn are infinite. As I designed projects for this book, I found that I was challenged and inspired by what I could do with a single skein. My intention was to create a collection of projects that are unique, fun, and best of all, quick to complete. The projects in *One Skein* provide an opportunity to try something new—to explore and experiment with a new stitch pattern or technique or perhaps learn about a fiber that you've always wanted to try. Those who seek instant gratification will find plenty of opportunities for completing projects quickly.

As I reflect on this collection, it's fun to see where experiences in my own life have shown up in the designs. At one point while I was working on the book, I was reading *Full Bloom: The Art and Life of Georgia O'Keeffe* by Hunter Drohojowska-Philp (Norton, 2004). I was intrigued to learn that one of O'Keeffe's close friends early in her career was photographer Paul Strand, well known for his abstract images. Was it their meeting and subsequent friendship that inspired Georgia to experiment with scale and proportion? How did the two people influence each other? Did reading this biography inspire me to create the Petal Bib? Or perhaps explain why I chose to adapt a delicate stitch pattern originally worked

with fingering-weight fiber and small gauge to a bulky yarn and large crochet hook for the Ruffle Cravat? While it may be difficult to define exactly where inspiration comes from, I love knowing that I may be inspired by the next book I read, a conversation with a friend, or a new skein of yarn, and I think it is inevitable that life's experiences work their way into our stitches, one project at a time.

I hope you enjoy exploring the possibilities that one skein of yarn can hold for you as much as I did. Think about walking around your favorite yarn shop or yarn department and discovering a new skein. Pick it up (okay, some of you may grab it excitedly) and think about the potential that yarn contains. The possibilities are endless. Have fun exploring the patterns in this book and discovering the promise of just one skein.

*1* | put it on

# LEG**warmers**

*Widely popular in the 1980s, leg warmers are making a comeback. And for good reason. Not only are they a great beginner knitting project, they really do keep your legs warm. This pair has a subtle rib at one end and a lace pattern at the other, with smooth stockinette stitch in between. Wear the lace panel at the top or bottom, and add a silk ribbon for a romantic touch.*

## FINISHED SIZE
About 9½" (24 cm) circumference and 13½" (34.5 cm) long.

## YARN
Sportweight (CYCA Fine #2) yarn.
*Shown here:* Louet Gems Opal (100% merino wool, 225 yd [206 m]/100 g): French blue.

## NEEDLES
Size 7 (4.5 mm): set of 4 or 5 double-pointed. Change needle size if necessary to obtain the correct gauge.

## NOTIONS
Marker (m); tapestry needle; two 22" (56 cm) lengths of ⅜" (1-cm) ribbon (optional).

## GAUGE
21 sts and 28 rows = 4" (10 cm) in St st worked in the rnd.

## LEG WARMERS

### Stitch Guide
*Lace Pattern* (multiple of 5 sts)
*Rnd 1:* *Yo, sl 1, k2tog, psso, yo, k2; rep from * to end of rnd.
*Rnd 2:* Knit.
Repeat Rnds 1 and 2 for pattern.

### Leg Warmer (make 2)
CO 50 sts onto 1 needle. Arrange sts as evenly as possible on 3 or 4 dpn, place marker (pm), and join for working in the rnd, being careful not to twist sts. Work Rnds 1 and 2 of lace pattern (see Stitch Guide) until piece measures 1¾" (4.5 cm) from CO. Change to St st and cont even until piece measures 12½" (31.5 cm) from CO. Change to rib and work as foll: *K4, p1; rep from * to end of rnd. Work k4, p1 rib as established until piece measures 13½" (34.5 cm) from CO. BO all sts in rib patt.

### Finishing
Weave in loose ends. Block to measurements. Thread ribbon through eyelets where lace patt meets St st, if desired.

# TANK**top**

*If you think that a single skein of yarn isn't enough for a tank top, here's proof that it's not only possible, but it can be done with flair. This top is made up of two identical side panels that are sewn together along the center front and center back. The knit side faces out on one panel; the purl side faces out on the other. The seams are conspicuously sewn on the outside.*

## FINISHED SIZE

30 (32, 34, 36)" (76 [81.5, 86.5, 91.5] cm) chest/bust circumference.

## YARN

Laceweight (CYCA Super Fine #1) yarn, used doubled.
*Shown here:* Lorna's Laces Helen's Lace (50% silk, 50% wool; 1250 yd [1143 m]/ 4 oz [114 g]): #ns16 charcoal in size 34" and #ns2 manzanita in size 36".

## NEEDLES

Size 8 (5 mm): straight. Change needle size if necessary to obtain the correct gauge.

## NOTIONS

Tapestry needle; size F/5 (3.75 mm) crochet hook.

## GAUGE

23 sts and 28 rows = 4" (10 cm) in St st with yarn doubled.

## TANK TOP

### Stitch Guide
*Seed Stitch*
*Row 1:* \*K1, p1; rep from \*, ending k1 if there is an odd number of sts.
*Row 2:* Knit the purl sts, and purl the knit sts as they appear.
*Row 3:* Rep Row 2.

### Notes
Yarn is used double throughout.

The center front and back have decorative seam allowances that use ¼" (6 mm) from each selvedge of the body panels. For blocking purposes, the measurements on the schematic show the actual size of the body panels, including seam allowances. However, the ½" (1.3 cm) of each panel consumed by the seams is not counted toward the finished chest/bust measurement.

### Panel A Front/Back
With double strand of yarn, CO 89 (95, 100, 106) sts. Work in seed st (see Stitch Guide) for 3 rows. Change to St st and work even until piece measures 14" (35.5 cm) from CO, ending with a WS row.
*Shape armhole:* (RS) K39 (42, 44, 47), join new ball of yarn and BO center 11 (11, 12, 12) sts, knit to end—39 (42, 44, 47) sts each side. Working each side separately, dec 1 st at each armhole edge (on either side of center BO gap) on the next WS row—38 (41, 43, 46) sts rem each side. Dec 1 st at each armhole edge every RS row 3 times—35 (38, 40, 43) sts rem each side. Work even until armhole measures 2½ (3, 3, 3½)" (6.5 [7.5, 7.5, 9] cm), ending with a WS row.
*Shape neck:* (RS) BO 19 (22, 24, 27) sts at beg of first section, knit to end of first section, knit all sts of second section. *Next row:* (WS) BO 19 (22, 24, 27) sts at beg of first section, purl to end of section; purl all sts of second section—16 sts rem each side for all sizes. Cont working each side separately, dec 1 st at each neck edge every RS row 4 times—12 sts rem each side. Cont even until armhole measures 6½ (7, 7, 7½)" (16.5 [18, 18, 19] cm). BO all sts.

## Panel B Front/Back

Work as for panel A.

## Finishing

Block pieces to measurements. Fold one body panel in half lengthwise with RS (knit side) tog. With doubled strand of yarn threaded on a tapestry needle, sew shoulder seam. Fold other body panel in half lengthwise with WS (purl side) tog, and sew shoulder seam with doubled strand of yarn; the knit side of the St st fabric will be the RS of one panel, and the purl side of the fabric will be the RS of the other panel.

*Center front and back seams:* With doubled strand of yarn threaded on a tapestry needle, and beg 2" (5 cm) up from CO to leave a slit at lower edge, use a backstitch (see Techniques, page 119) to sew the two panels tog at center front and back with a ¼" (6 mm) seam allowance on the RS side of the garment. Rep for other center seam, sewing all the way from CO edge to neck, without leaving a slit.

*Edging:* With doubled strand of yarn and crochet hook, work single crochet (see Techniques, page 114) around neck and armhole openings.

Weave in loose ends.

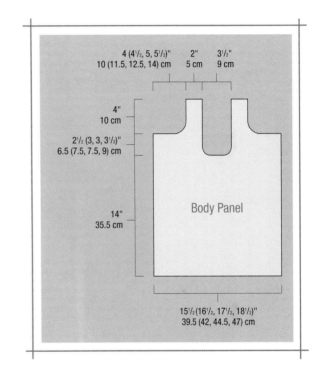

4 (4½, 5, 5½)"
10 (11.5, 12.5, 14) cm   2"   3½"
                          5 cm   9 cm

4"
10 cm

2½ (3, 3, 3½)"
6.5 (7.5, 7.5, 9) cm

14"
35.5 cm

Body Panel

15½ (16½, 17½, 18½)"
39.5 (42, 44.5, 47) cm

# CABLE**footies**

Typically, I don't like to wear
socks. However, there are times
when I need something on my feet.
This pair of footies is perfect for
wearing around the house on a
cold morning. The foot is knitted
in a thick and cozy cable pattern,
but the leg stops at the ankle. The
footies are quick to knit, and you'll
find that you'll want a pair in all
your favorite colors.

## FINISHED SIZE
About 8 (8½, 9)" (20.5 [21.5, 23] cm) foot circumference and 9½ (10, 10½)" (24 [25.5, 26.5] cm) long from back of heel to tip of toe. To fit women's U.S. shoe sizes 7½–8½ (9–10, 10½–11); largest size will also fit men's U.S. shoe sizes 9–10.

## YARN
Worsted-weight (CYCA Medium #4) yarn.
*Shown here:* Lorna's Laces Shepherd Worsted (100% superwash wool, 225 yd [206 m]/4 oz): #45 NS cranberry.

## NEEDLES
Size 8 (5 mm): set of 4 or 5 double-pointed (dpn). Change needle size if necessary to obtain the correct gauge.

## NOTIONS
Markers (m); cable needle (cn); tapestry needle.

## GAUGE
18 sts and 26 rows = 4" (10 cm) in St st worked in the rnd; 22-st cable patt for instep measures 2¾" (7 cm) wide with cables relaxed.

# CABLE FOOTIES

## Stitch Guide
*Left Cable (LC)* (worked over 4 sts)
Slip 2 sts onto cn and hold in front, k2, k2 from cn.

*Cable Pattern for Leg* (multiple of 6 sts)
*Rnds 1 and 2:* *K4, p2; rep from * to end of rnd.
*Rnd 3:* *LC, p2; rep from * to end of rnd.
*Rnds 4 and 5:* Rep Rnds 1 and 2.
Repeat Rnds 1–5 for pattern.

*Cable Pattern for Instep* (worked over 22 sts)
*Rnds 1 and 2:* [K4, p2] 3 times, k4.
*Rnd 3:* [LC, p2] 3 times, LC.
*Rnds 4 and 5:* Rep Rnds 1 and 2.
Repeat Rnds 1–5 for pattern.

## Leg
CO 48 sts onto 1 needle for all sizes. Divide sts as evenly as possible on 3 or 4 dpn, place marker (pm), and join for working in the rnd, being careful not to twist sts. Rep Rnds 1–5 of cable patt for leg (see Stitch Guide) until piece measures about 2" (5 cm) from CO, ending with Rnd 5 of patt.

## Heel
*Heel flap:* K10, p2tog, turn work. P23, p2tog—24 heel sts.

Place rem 22 sts on spare needle to be worked later for instep; the first and last 4 instep sts should be 4-st cable columns. Work 24 heel sts back and forth in rows as foll:
*Row 1:* (RS) *Sl 1 kwise with yarn in back (wyb), k1; rep from * to end of row.
*Row 2:* (WS) *Sl 1 pwise with yarn in front (wyf), p1; rep from * to end of row.
Rep Rows 1 and 2 until a total of 22 (24, 26) heel flap rows have been worked, ending with Row 2— 11 (12, 13) chain edge sts at each selvedge.

*Turn heel:* (worked the same for all sizes) Work short-rows to shape heel as foll:

*Row 1:* (RS) K14, ssk, k1, turn.

*Row 2:* Sl 1 pwise wyf, p5, p2tog, p1, turn.

*Row 3:* Sl 1 pwise wyb, knit to 1 st before gap formed by turn on previous row, ssk, k1, turn.

*Row 4:* Sl 1 pwise wyf, purl to 1 st before gap formed by turn on previous row, p2tog, p1, turn.

Repeat Rows 3 and 4 until all heel sts have been worked, ending with a WS row—14 heel sts rem.

*Gusset:* Resume working in the rnd as foll: With Needle 1, k14 heel sts, then pick up and knit 12 (13, 14) sts along selvedge of heel flap (chain selvedge sts, plus 1 extra st in corner); with Needle 2, work Rnd 1 of cable patt for instep (see Stitch Guide) over 22 instep sts; with Needle 3, pick up and knit 12 (13, 14) sts along other selvedge edge of heel flap, then knit the first 7 heel sts again—60 (62, 64) sts: 19 (20, 21) sts each on Needles 1 and 3; 22 instep sts on Needle 2. Rnd now begins at center back heel.

*Rnd 1:* On Needle 1, knit to last 3 sts, k2tog, k1; on Needle 2, work 22 instep sts in established cable patt; on Needle 3, k1, ssk, knit to end—2 sts dec'd.

*Rnd 2:* Knit.

Rep Rnds 1 and 2 six more times—46 (48, 50) sts rem: 12 (13, 14) sts each on Needles 1 and 3; 22 instep sts on Needle 2.

## Foot

Work even in established patt until piece measures 6½ (7, 7¼)" (16.5 [18, 18.5] cm) from back of heel, or about 3 (3, 3¼)" (7.5 [7.5, 8.5] cm) less than desired total foot length, ending with Rnd 5 of cable patt.

*For smallest size only:* Knit 1 rnd, dec 1 st each on Needles 1 and 3—44 sts rem; 11 sts each on Needles 1 and 3; 22 sts on Needle 2.

*For medium size only:* Without working any sts, move last st from Needle 1 onto Needle 2, and move first st from Needle 3 onto Needle 2—still 48 sts: 12 st each on Needles 1 and 3; 24 sts on Needle 2.

*For largest size only:* Knit 1 rnd, dec 1 st each on Needles 1 and 3—48 sts rem; 13 sts each on Needles 1 and 3; 22 sts on Needle 2. Without working any sts, move last st from Needle 1 onto Needle 2, and move first st from Needle 3 onto Needle 2—still 48 sts: 12 st each on Needles 1 and 3; 24 sts on Needle 2.

## Toe

*Rnd 1:* On Needle 1, knit to last 3 sts, k2tog, k1; Needle 2, k1, ssk, work to last 3 sts, k2tog, k1; on Needle 3, k1 ssk, knit to end—4 sts dec'd.

*Rnd 2:* Knit.

Rep Rnds 1 and 2 eight (nine, nine) more times—8 sts rem for all sizes. Divide sts so that there are 4 sts each on 2 needles. Cut yarn, leaving a 12" (30.5-cm) tail. Thread tail on a tapestry needle and use the Kitchener st (see Techniques, page 120) to graft rem sts tog.

## Finishing

Weave in loose ends. Block lightly, if desired.

# SILK sleeves

*I love the combination of silk and mohair in this feathery light yarn, and I use it so often, by itself or in combination with other yarns, that my friends are beginning to tease me. Despite their "Not agains!" I still find the yarn ideal for many projects, especially ones worked in plain stockinette stitch. Wear the sleeves with your favorite out-fit—jeans and a tank top or a little black dress—when you want to take the chill off your arms.*

## FINISHED SIZE

About 10" (25.5 cm) circumference at upper arm, 7½" (19 cm) circumference at cuff, and 28½" (72.5 cm) long.

## YARN

Fingering-weight (CYCA Super Fine #1) yarn. *Shown here:* Rowan Kidsilk Haze (70% kid mohair, 30% silk; 229 yd [209 m]/25 g): #600 dewberry (lilac) and #583 blushes (rose).

## NEEDLES

Size 9 (5.5 mm). Change needle size if necessary to obtain the correct gauge.

## NOTIONS

Tapestry needle.

## GAUGE

15 sts and 21 rows = 4" (10 cm) in St st.

## SILK SLEEVES

### Sleeve (make 2)

CO 28 sts. Beg with a WS row, work even in St st for 13 rows. *Inc row:* (RS) Inc 1 st each end of needle—2 sts inc'd. Rep the last 14 rows 4 more times—38 sts. Cont even until piece measures 28½" (72.5 cm) from CO, or desired length. Using the sewn method (see Techniques, page 113), BO all sts.

### Finishing

With yarn threaded on a tapestry needle, sew sleeve seam. Weave in loose ends. Block lightly.

# UNISEX**gloves**

*Many beginning knitters wonder if gloves are worth the effort of knitting all those fingers. I, too, considered gloves to be too much work. But that was before I made myself a pair several years ago. There is something luxurious and special about handknitted gloves— they just don't compare to anything you can buy.*

## UNISEX GLOVES

### Stitch Guide
*Cuff Pattern* (multiple of 8 sts)
*Rnd 1 and all odd-numbered rnds:* Knit.
*Rnd 2:* *Sl 2 sts onto cn and hold in back of work, k2, k2 from cn, sl 2 sts onto cn and hold in front of work, k2, k2 from cn; rep from * to end of rnd.
*Rnds 4 and 6:* Knit.
*Rnd 8:* *Sl 2 sts onto cn and hold in front, k2, k2 from cn, sl 2 sts onto cn and hold in back, k2, k2 from cn; rep from * to end of rnd.
*Rnd 10:* Knit.
Repeat Rnds 1–10 for pattern.

### Note
Both gloves have the same shaping and can be worn on either hand.

### Cuff
With larger needles, CO 40 (48, 56) sts onto 1 dpn. Distribute sts evenly on 4 dpn, place marker (pm), and join for working in the rnd, being careful not to twist sts. Work Rnds 1–10 of cuff pattern (see Stitch Guide) 1 (2, 2) times, then work Rnds 1–2 once more—cuff should measure about 1½ (3, 3)" (3.8 [7.5, 7.5] cm) from CO.

### Hand
Change to smaller needles and St st. Knit 1 rnd, dec 7 (9, 11) sts evenly spaced—33 (39, 45) sts rem. Knit 1 rnd even.
*Thumb gusset:* Establish position of thumb gusset on next rnd as foll: K16 (19, 22), pm, M1L (see Techniques, page 118), k1, M1R (see Techniques, page 118), pm, k16 (19, 22)—3 gusset sts between markers; 35 (41, 47) sts total. Knit 1 rnd even. *Inc rnd:* Knit to first gusset marker, slip marker (sl m), M1L, knit to next gusset marker, M1R, sl m, knit to end—2 gusset sts inc'd. Knit 1 rnd even, then work inc rnd once more—7 gusset sts between markers. Knit 2 rnds even, then work inc rnd once more—9 gusset sts between markers. Rep the last 3 rnds 1 (2, 3) more

### FINISHED SIZE
About 6¼ (7½, 8½)" (16 [19, 21.5] cm) hand circumference. To fit a child (woman, man).

### YARN
Worsted-weight (CYCA Medium #4) yarn.
*Shown here:* Araucania Nature Wool (100% wool; 242 yd [220 m]/100 g): #20 green (child), #17 red (woman), and #09 brown (man).

### NEEDLES
Cuff: size 7 (4.5 mm): set of 5 double-pointed (dpn). Hand and fingers: size 6 (4 mm): set of 5 dpn. Change needle size if necessary to obtain the correct gauge.

### NOTIONS
Markers (m); cable needle (cn); stitch holders or waste yarn; tapestry needle.

### GAUGE
21 sts and 28 rows = 4" (10 cm) in St st worked in the round on smaller needles for hand and fingers.

time(s)—11 (13, 15) gusset sts between markers; 43 (51, 59) sts total—glove should measure about 1¾ (2¼, 2¾)" (4.5 [5.5, 7] cm) from beg of St st section, or about 3¼ (5¼, 5¾)" (8.5 [13.5, 14.5] cm) from CO. *Next rnd:* Knit to first gusset marker, remove m, place 11 (13, 15) gusset sts onto holder or waste yarn, remove second gusset m, use the backward loop method (see Techniques, page 113) to CO 1 st over gap left by gusset sts, knit to end—33 (39, 45) sts. Work even in St st until piece measures 3 (3¾, 4½)" (7.5 [9.5, 11.5] cm) from beg of St st section.

*Little finger:* K4 (5, 6), place next 25 (29, 33) sts onto holder or waste yarn, use the backward loop method to CO 1 st over gap, knit rem 4 (5, 6) sts of rnd—9 (11, 13) little finger sts. Arrange sts as evenly as possible on 3 dpn. Work even in St st until finger measures 1½ (2¼, 2¾)" (3.8 [5.5, 7] cm).

*Shape top:* *K2tog; rep from * to last 3 sts, k3tog—4 (5, 6) sts rem. Break yarn, thread tail through rem sts, pull tight, and fasten off.

*Upper hand:* Return 25 (29, 33) held sts to dpn and join yarn with RS facing to beg of st CO at base of little finger. Pick up and knit 2 (2, 3) sts across base of little finger, knit to end—27 (31, 36) sts. Work 1 more rnd even in St st—piece measures ¼" (6 mm) from base of little finger.

*Ring finger:* Place first 4 (5, 6) sts and last 5 (5, 6) sts of rnd onto dpn, and place rem 18 (21, 24) sts on holder to work later. Join yarn to sts at beg of rnd with RS facing. Knit first 4 (5, 6) sts, use the backward loop method to CO 1 (2, 2) st(s) over gap, knit last 5 (5, 6) sts—10 (12, 14) sts total. Work even in St st until finger measures 2 (3, 3¼)" (5 [7.5, 8.5] cm).

*Shape top:* *K2tog; rep from * to end of rnd—5 (6, 7) sts rem. Finish as for little finger.

*Middle finger:* Place first 5 (5, 6) sts and last 4 (5, 6) sts of rnd onto dpn, and place rem 9 (11, 12) sts on holder to work later. Join yarn to beg of st(s) CO at base of ring finger with RS facing. Pick up and knit 2 sts from st(s) CO at base of ring finger, knit first 5 (5, 6) sts, use the backward loop method to CO 1 st over gap, knit last 4 (5, 6) sts—12 (13, 15) sts. Work even in St st until finger measures 2¼ (3¼, 3½)" (5.5 [8.5, 9] cm).

*Shape top:* *K2tog; rep from * to last 0 (3, 3) sts, k3tog 0 (1, 1) time—6 (6, 7) sts rem. Finish as for little finger.

*Index finger:* Place rem 9 (11, 12) sts onto dpn, and join yarn with RS facing to beg of st CO at base of middle finger. Pick up and knit 2 (1, 2) st(s) from st CO at base of middle finger, knit to end—11 (12, 14) sts total. Work even in St st until finger measures 2 (3, 3¼)" (5 [7.5, 8.5] cm).

*Shape top:* *K2tog; rep from * to last 3 (0, 0) sts, k3tog 1 (0, 0) time—5 (6, 7) sts rem. Finish as for little finger.

## Thumb

Place 11 (13, 15) held gusset sts onto dpn, and join yarn with RS facing to beg of st CO at thumb gap. Pick up and knit 1 st from st CO at gap, knit to end—12 (14, 16) sts total. Work even in St st until thumb measures 1½ (2, 2½)" (3.8 [5, 6.5] cm).

*Shape top:* *K2tog; rep from * to end of rnd—6 (7, 8) sts rem. Finish as for little finger.

## Finishing

Weave in loose ends, using yarn tails to close any gaps at base of fingers and thumb. Block to measurements.

# ASYMMETRICAL
# CABLE**hat**

Sometimes I can't settle on a single stitch pattern. That indecision turned into serendipity when I combined wide and narrow cables with ribs in this asymmetrical hat design. It's knitted in the round with no crown shaping, and you'll have it off your needles and on your head in just a few hours.

## FINISHED SIZE

About 15 (16¼, 17, 17¾)" (38 [41.5, 43, 45] cm) circumference with fabric relaxed; will stretch up to 19 (20¼, 21½, 22¾)" (48.5 [51.5, 54.5, 58] cm). To fit a toddler (child, woman, man).

## YARN

Chunky-weight (CYCA Bulky #5) yarn.
*Shown here:* Rowan Polar (60% wool, 30% alpaca, 10% acrylic; 109 yd [100 m]/100 g): #650 smirk (pale lavender) and #655 combat (dark gray), both in size 17".

## NEEDLES

Size 11 (8 mm): 16" or 24" (40 or 60 cm) circular (cir). Change needle size if necessary to obtain the correct gauge.

## NOTIONS

Marker (m); cable needle (cn); tapestry needle; 1½ × 3" (3.8 × 7.5 cm) piece of cardboard (for pom-pom, optional).

## GAUGE

17 sts and 17 rnds = 4" (10 cm) in k1, p2 rib, worked in the rnd with rib relaxed.

## ASYMMETRICAL CABLE HAT

### Hat

CO 63 (69, 72, 75) sts. Place marker (pm) and join for working in the rnd, being careful not to twist sts. Rep Rnds 1–8 of Cables chart until piece measures 7 (8, 9, 10)" (18 [20.5, 23, 25.5] cm) from CO. BO all sts, leaving a 20" (51-cm) tail.

### Finishing

Turn hat inside out (RS facing tog), and lay it out flat. With yarn threaded on a tapestry needle, sew straight across top edge, from fold line to fold line. Turn hat right side out. Bring corners of hat together sew them securely to each other, point to point.
*Pom-pom:* Following the instructions on page 118, make a 3" (7.5-cm) pom-pom. Fasten pom-pom to top of hat where corners are joined. Weave in loose ends.

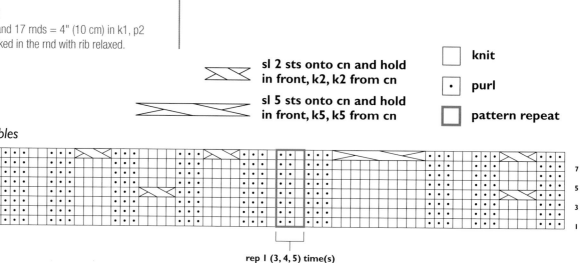

sl 2 sts onto cn and hold in front, k2, k2 from cn

sl 5 sts onto cn and hold in front, k5, k5 from cn

☐ knit

⊡ purl

☐ pattern repeat

*Cables*

7

5

3

1

rep 1 (3, 4, 5) time(s)

# RIB & CABLE
## quartet

Each scarf in this collection features
a different combination of ribs
and cables for you to explore. The
scarves vary in width and length,
but all are knitted with buttery
soft organic cotton yarn that is
comfortable against even the most
sensitive skin. The gaiter, worked
in the round with a silk-alpaca
yarn, feels fabulous as it provides
extra warmth around your neck.

## FINISHED SIZES

Single Cable Scarf: About 3" (7.5 cm) wide and 50" (127 cm) long.
Double Cable Scarf: About 3¾" (9.5 cm) wide and 38" (96.5 cm) long.
Triple Cable Muffler: About 5" (12.5 cm) wide and 26" (66 cm) long.
Gaiter: About 20" (51 cm) circumference and 4¼" (11 cm) high.

## YARN

Worsted-weight (Medium #4) yarn.
*Shown here:*
Scarves: Blue Sky Alpacas Organic Cotton (100% organic cotton, 150 yd [137 m]/ 100 g): #80 bone for Single Cable Scarf; #82 nut (medium brown) for Double Cable Scarf, and #83 sage for Triple Cable Muffler.
Gaiter: Blue Sky Alpacas Alpaca & Silk (50% alpaca, 50% silk; 146 yd [133 m] /100 g): #i00 slate.

## NEEDLES

Scarves: Size 9 (5.5 mm).
Gaiter: size 6 (4 mm): 16" (40-cm) circular (cir). Change needle size if necessary to obtain the correct gauge.

## NOTIONS

Marker (m; for gaiter only); cable needle (cn); tapestry needle.

## GAUGE

Scarves: 28 sts and 20 rows = 4" (10 cm) in k2, p2 rib on size 9 (5.5 mm) needles, with rib relaxed.
Gaiter: 35 sts and 29 rows = 4" (10 cm) in k2, p2 rib on size 6 (4 mm) needles, with rib relaxed.

# RIB AND CABLE QUARTET

## Stitch Guide
### Selvedge Stitches
Slip the first and last stitches as if to knit (kwise) with yarn in back on all RS rows; and purl the first and last stitches on all WS rows.

### 4/4 Left Cable
(worked over 8 sts) Sl 4 sts onto cn and hold in front of work, k4, k3 from cn, sl last st from cn kwise.

### 3/3 Left Cable
(worked over 6 sts) Sl 3 sts onto cn and hold in front of work, k3, k3 from cn.

### 3/3 Right Cable
(worked over 6 sts) Sl 3 sts onto cn and hold in back of work, k3, k3 from cn.

## Single Cable Scarf
*Shown on page 34.*
CO 21 sts. *Set-up row:* (WS) P8, [k2, p2] 3 times, p1. Cont in rib and cable patt as foll:
*Rows 1, 3, and 7:* (RS) Sl 1 kwise, [k2, p2] 3 times, k7, sl 1 kwise.
*Rows 2, 4, and 6:* P8, [k2, p2] 3 times, p1.
*Row 5:* Sl 1 kwise, [k2, p2] 3 times, work 4/4 left cable (see Stitch Guide) over last 8 sts.
Rep Rows 1–8 (do not rep set-up row) until piece measures 50" (127 cm) from CO, ending with Row 3 of patt. BO all sts in patt. Weave in loose ends. Block to measurements.

## Double Cable Scarf
*Shown on page 32.*
CO 28 sts. *Set-up row:* (WS) P3, *k2, p2; rep from * to last st, p1. Cont in k2, p2 rib patt as foll:
*Row 1:* (RS) Sl 1 kwise, k2, *p2, k2; rep from * to last st, sl 1 kwise.
*Row 2:* P3, *k2, p2; rep from * to last st, p1.

Rep Rows 1 and 2 (do not rep set-up row) until piece measures 2" (5 cm) from CO, ending with a RS row. Set up cable patt row as foll: (WS) P3, *k2, p6, k2, p2; rep from * once, p1. Cont in cable patt as foll:

*Row 1:* (RS) Sl 1 kwise, k2, *p2, work 3/3 left cable (see Stitch Guide) over next 6 sts, p2, k2; rep from * once, sl 1 kwise.

*Rows 2, 4, and 6:* P3, *k2, p6, k2, p2; rep from * once, p1.

*Rows 3 and 5:* Sl 1 kwise, k2, *p2, k6, p2, k2; rep from * once, sl 1 kwise.

Rep Rows 1–6 of cable patt seven more times, then work Row 1 once more—9 cable crossing rows; piece measures about 12" (30.5 cm) from CO. Work set-up row for k2, p2 rib as for beg of scarf, then cont in k2, p2 rib until piece measures 26" (66 cm) from CO edge, ending with a RS row. Work set-up row of cable patt on next WS row, then substituting 3/3 right cable (see Stitch Guide) for 3/3 left cable, rep Rows 1–6 of cable patt 8 times, then work Row 1 once more—9 cable crossing rows at this end of scarf; piece measures about 36" (91.5 cm) from CO. Work set-up row for k2, p2 rib as for beg of scarf, then cont in k2, p2 rib for 2"

(5 cm)—piece measures 38" (96.5 cm) from CO. BO all sts in rib. Weave in loose ends. Block to measurements.

## Triple Cable Muffler

*Shown on this page and page 33.*

CO 40 sts. Work set-up row for k2, p2 rib as foll: (WS) P3, *k2, p2; rep from * to last st, p1. Cont in k2, p2 rib patt as foll:

*Row 1:* (RS) Sl 1 kwise, k2, *p2, k2; rep from * to last st, sl 1 kwise.

*Row 2:* P3, *k2, p2; rep from * to last st, p1.

Rep Rows 1 and 2 until piece measures 1¾" (4.5 cm) from CO, ending with a RS row. Work cable patt set-up row as foll: (WS) P3, *k2, p6, k2, p2; rep from * to last st, p1. Cont in cable patt as foll:

*Row 1:* (RS) Sl 1 kwise, k2, *p2, work 3/3 left cable (see Stitch Guide) over next 6 sts, p2, k2; rep from * to last st, sl 1 kwise.

*Rows 2 and 4:* P3, *k2, p6, k2, p2; rep from * to last st, p1.

*Row 3:* Sl 1 kwise, k2, *p2, k6, p2, k2; rep from * to last st, sl 1 kwise.

Rep Rows 1–4 of cable patt once more, then work Row 1 again—3 cable crossing rows; piece measures about 3¾" (9.5 cm) from CO edge. Work set-up row for k2, p2 rib as for beg of scarf, then cont in k2, p2 rib until piece measures 22¼" (56.5 cm) from CO edge, ending with a RS row. Work set-up row of cable patt on next WS row, then substituting 3/3 right cable (see Stitch Guide) for 3/3 left cable, rep Rows 1–4 of cable once, then work Row 1 once more—3 cable crossing rows at this end of scarf; piece measures about 24¼" (61.5 cm) from CO. Work set-up row for k2, p2 rib as for beg of scarf, then cont in k2, p2 rib for 1¾" (4.5 cm)—piece measures about 26" (66 cm) from CO edge. BO all sts in rib. Weave in loose ends. Block to measurements.

## Gaiter

With cir needle, CO 176 sts. Place marker (pm) and join for working in the rnd, being careful not to twist sts. Establish k2, p2 rib as foll: *K2, p2; rep from * to end. Work k2, p2 rib until piece measures 1¼" (3.2 cm) from CO.

*Cable set-up rnd:* *[K2, p2] 3 times, [k6, p2, k2, p2] 2 times, k6, p2; rep from * 3 more times.

*Rnd 1:* *[K2, p2] 3 times, [work 3/3 left cable (see Stitch Guide) over next 6 sts, p2, k2, p2] 2 times, work 3/3 left cable over next 6 sts, p2; rep from * 3 more times.

*Rnds 2–4:* *[K2, p2] 3 times, [k6, p2, k2, p2] 2 times, k6, p2; rep from * 3 more times.

Rep Rnds 1–4 two more times (do not rep cable set-up rnd), then work Rnd 1 of cable patt once more—4 cable crossing rnds; piece measures about 3" (7.5 cm) from CO. Change to k2, p2 rib as for beg of piece. Work in k2, p2 rib for 1¼" (3.2 cm)—piece measures about 4¼" (11 cm) from CO. BO all sts in rib.

Weave in loose ends. Block lightly to measurements.

# FINGERLESS
# GARTER**mitts**

*Keep your hands fashionably warm in a pair of fingerless mitts. Super-simple, they're worked side to side in garter stitch, then seamed along the inside of the hand with a custom-fit thumb opening. A few rows of elongated stitches make the knitting conform to the shape of your hand and give the mitts a lacy look. Add beads or even sequins (it's easy!) for a dressy alternative.*

## FINISHED SIZE

About 6" (15 cm) circumference with fabric relaxed and 7" (18 cm) long; will stretch to fit up to 8" (20.5 cm) circumference.

## YARN

Sportweight (CYCA Fine #2) yarn.
*Shown here:* Koigu Premium Merino (100% wool; 170 yd [156 m]/50 g): #2343 light green for plain version; #1220 red for beaded version.

## NEEDLES

Size 1 (2.25 mm). Change needle size if necessary to obtain the correct gauge.

## NOTIONS

112 (56 for each hand) size 8 seed beads; Big Eye beading needle (available at craft and bead stores); tapestry needle.

## GAUGE

32 sts and 64 rows = 4" (10 cm) in garter st.

## FINGERLESS GARTER MITTS

### Note

Slip the first stitch of every row knitwise.

### Beaded Version

*Left Mitt:* With beading needle, thread 56 seed beads onto yarn. Slide beads down along the yarn away from the work as needed. With beaded strand of yarn, CO 55 sts. Slipping the first st of each row (see Note), work in garter st for 10 rows (5 ridges), ending with a WS row.

*Row 1:* (RS) Sl 1, k2, knit the next 27 sts wrapping the yarn twice around the needle for each st, k25 in the usual manner.

*Row 2:* Knit, dropping the extra wrap for each of the double-wrapped sts to create elongated sts.

*Rows 3–6:* Knit.

*Row 7:* (RS) Sl 1, k2, knit the next 27 sts wrapping the yarn three times around the needle for each st, k25 in the usual manner.

*Row 8:* Knit, dropping the extra wraps for each triple-wrapped st to create even taller elongated sts.

*Row 9:* Knit.

*Row 10:* (bead row; WS) Sl 1, k25, [slide bead into place close to needle, k2] 14 times, k1.

*Rows 11–13:* Knit.

*Row 14:* (bead row) Rep Row 10.

*Row 15:* Rep Row 1.

*Row 16:* (bead row) Rep Row 10, dropping the extra wrap for each double-wrapped st.

*Rows 17–19:* Knit.

*Row 20:* (bead row) Rep Row 10.

*Row 21:* Rep Row 7.

*Rows 22–26:* Knit, dropping the extra wraps for each triple-wrapped st in Row 21.

*Row 27:* Rep Row 1.

Knit 59 more rows, dropping the extra wrap for each double-wrapped st in first row—30 garter ridges above last elongated row; piece measures about 6" (15 cm) from CO, measured along the plain garter st section for wrist, and slightly longer in beaded and elongated st section for hand. BO all sts, leaving a 12" (30.5-cm) tail. With tail threaded on a tapestry needle, sew side seam, leaving a 2" (5-cm) opening for thumb in center of seam, or wherever best fit for thumb is achieved. Weave in loose ends.

*Right Mitt:* With beading needle, thread 56 seed beads onto yarn. With beaded strand of yarn, CO 55 sts. Slipping the first st of each row, work in garter st for 10 rows (5 ridges), ending with a WS row.

*Row 1:* (RS) Sl 1, k24, knit the next 27 sts wrapping the yarn twice around the needle for each st, k3 in the usual manner.

*Row 2:* Knit, dropping the extra wrap for each of the double-wrapped sts to create elongated sts.

*Rows 3–6:* Knit.

*Row 7:* (RS) Sl 1, k24, knit the next 27 sts wrapping the yarn three times around the needle for each st, k3 in the usual manner.

*Row 8:* Knit, dropping the extra wraps for each triple-wrapped st to create even taller elongated sts.

*Row 9:* Knit.

*Row 10:* (bead row; WS) Sl 1, [k2, slide bead into place close to needle] 14 times, k26.

*Rows 11–13:* Knit.

*Row 14:* (bead row) Rep Row 10.

*Row 15:* Rep Row 1.

*Row 16:* (bead row) Rep Row 10, dropping the extra wrap for each double-wrapped st.

*Rows 17–19:* Knit.

*Row 20:* (bead row) Rep Row 10.

*Row 21:* Rep Row 7.

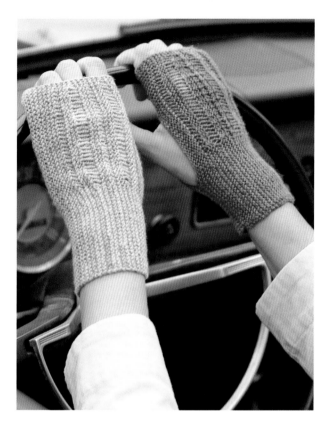

*Rows 22–26:* Knit, dropping the extra wraps for each triple-wrapped st in Row 21.

*Row 27:* Rep Row 1.

Knit 59 more rows, dropping the extra wrap for each double-wrapped st in first row—30 garter ridges above last elongated row; piece measures about 6" (15 cm) from CO measured along the section without beads or elongated sts. BO all sts, leaving a 12" (30.5-cm) tail. Finish as for left mitt. Weave in loose ends.

## Plain Version

Work as for beaded version, but do not string beads on yarn before beginning, and work all bead rows as sl 1, knit to end.

# CROCHETcap & RUFFLEcravat

*This quick and easy hat begins at the top and progresses in ever-widening circles in single crochet. A decorative edging finishes off the brim. The coordinating ruffle-like cravat is worked in a series of partial circles in the Scalloped Braid pattern from Mon Tricot, 250 Knit and Crochet Patterns (Crown Publications, 1977). This pattern was originally presented as a delicate edging worked with fingering-weight yarn, but it takes on an entirely different look when it's worked in bulky yarn. The scallops hook on one another to hold the cravat closed.*

## CROCHET CAP AND RUFFLE CRAVAT

**Note**

See Techniques, page 114, for basic crochet instructions.

### Cap

With larger hook, ch 3. Join with a sl st to form a ring. Using a marker to indicate end of each rnd and repositioning marker as necessary, cont in rnds as foll:

*Rnd 1:* Ch 1 (counts as 1 sc), work 7 sc in ring, join with a sl st—8 sc.

*Rnd 2:* Ch 1 (counts as 1 sc), sc in top of starting ch-1 of previous rnd, 2 sc in each st of previous rnd, join with a sl st to top of ch-1 at beg of rnd—16 sc.

*Rnd 3:* Ch 1 (counts as 1 sc), sc in each sc of previous rnd.

*Rnd 4:* Ch 1 (counts as 1 sc), sc in top of starting ch-1 of previous rnd, 2 sc in each sc of previous rnd, join with a sl st to top of ch-1 at beg of rnd—32 sc.

*Rnd 5:* Ch 1 (counts as 1 sc), sc in each sc from previous rnd.

*Rnd 6:* Ch 1 (counts as 1 sc), *2 sc in next st, 1 sc in next st; rep from * to starting ch-1, sc in top of starting ch-1 of previous rnd, 2 sc in next sc, *2 sc in next sc, 1 sc in foll sc; rep from * to last 2 sc, work 2 sc in each of last 2 sc, join with a sl st to top of ch-1 at beg of rnd—50 sc.

Cont sc in rnds, working ch 1 at beg of each rnd, 1 sc in each sc, and joining end of each rnd with a sl st, until piece measures 5½" (14 cm) from beg.

*Edging:* Change to smaller hook and sl st to top of beg ch of previous row. Ch 4, [skip 2 sc, 3 dc in next st] 16 times, skip 1 sc, 2 dc in next st, join with a sl to 2nd ch of ch-4 at beg of rnd. Fasten off.

Weave in loose ends.

### Cravat

With larger hook, ch 4, sl st into first ch to form ring. Cont as foll:

*Row 1:* Ch 2, work 10 dc in ring. Turn.

*Row 2:* Ch 2, [dc in dc of previous row, ch 1] 10 times, dc in last st of previous row, sc in center of ring. Turn.

*Row 3:* Ch 1, [4 hdc in next ch-1 space (sp), sc in next sp] 5 times, ch 3, sc in same space as last sc—1 motif completed. Turn.

---

### FINISHED SIZE

Cap: About 20" (51 cm) circumference. Cravat: About 5½" (14 cm) wide and 26" (66 cm) long.

### YARN

Chunky-weight (CYCA Bulky #5) yarn.
*Shown here:* Debbie Bliss Cashmerino Superchunky (55% merino wool, 33% microfiber, 12% cashmere; 82 yd [75 m]/100 g): Cap shown in #10 deep rose and #15 tan; Cravat shown in #10 deep rose.

### HOOK

Cap and Cravat: size P/16 (11.5 mm). Cap edging: size H/8 (5 mm). Change hook size if necessary to obtain the correct gauge.

### NOTIONS

Stitch marker (m); tapestry needle.

### GAUGE

Cap: 10 sc and 13 rnds = 4" (10 cm) worked in the rnd using larger hook.
Cravat: 11 sc and 13 rows = 4" (10 cm) worked in rows using larger hook.

*Row 4:* Ch 2, work 10 dc in ch-3 loop at end of previous row. Turn.

*Row 5:* Ch 3, [dc in dc of previous row, ch 1] 9 times, dc in next dc, sc in center ring of previous motif. Turn.

*Row 6:* [4 hdc in next ch-1 sp, sc in next sp] 4 times, 4 hdc in next ch-1 sp, sc in top of ch of previous row, ch 3, sc in same space as last sc. Turn.

Rep Rows 4–6 seven more times, then work Rows 4 and 5 once again. *Last row:* [4 hdc in next ch-1 sp, sc in next sp] 4 times, 4 hdc in next sp, sc in top of ch of previous row. Fasten off—10 motifs completed; piece measures about 26" (66 cm) from beg, with motifs laid flat. Fasten off.

## Finishing

Cut yarn and thread tail on a tapestry needle. Sew edges of first and last motifs to adjacent motifs as shown by arrows in illustration at right. Weave in loose ends.

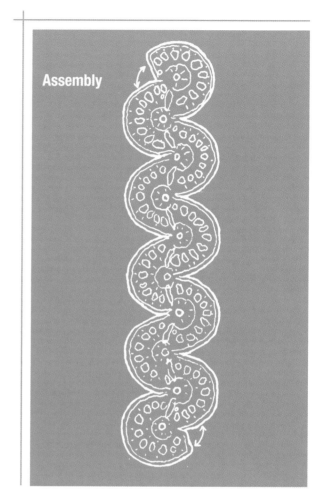

**Assembly**

2|take it with you

# THE**clutch** YOU'LL NEVER GIVE UP

*Forget bulky bags and purses—this felted clutch is big enough to carry the essentials without getting in the way. It is knitted in the round with bulky yarn, then felted down to a compact size. An assortment of buttons—I used a mixture of vintage and modern ones—gives it a unique personality. Short on buttons? Check out antique or thrift stores for unusual finds, or see page 124 for my favorite sources.*

## FINISHED SIZE

About 13" (33 cm) wide and 10¾" (27.5 cm) tall before felting; 10" (25.5 cm) wide and 6¼" (16 cm) tall after felting.

## YARN

Chunky-weight (CYCA Bulky #5) yarn. *Shown here:* Brown Sheep Lamb's Pride Bulky (85% wool, 15% mohair; 125 yd [114 m]/4 oz [114 g]): #102 orchid twist.

## NEEDLES

Size 15 (10 mm): 24" (60-cm) circular (cir). Change needle size if necessary to obtain the correct gauge.

## NOTIONS

Stitch marker (m); tapestry needle; 18 buttons (9 for each side) ranging in size from ⅜" (1 cm) to ½" (1.3 cm); sewing needle and matching thread (for attaching buttons).

## GAUGE

10 sts and 13 rows = 4" (10 cm) in St st worked in the rnd, before felting.

## THE CLUTCH YOU'LL NEVER GIVE UP

### Bag

CO 60 sts. Place marker (pm) and join for working in the rnd, being careful not to twist sts; rnd begins at side of bag. Knit 12 rnds, placing another marker after the 30th st on the first rnd to indicate other side of bag. *Inc rnd:* K1, knit into front and back of next st (k1f&b), knit to 2 sts before next m, k1f&b, k1, slip marker (sl m), k1, k1f&b, knit to 2 sts before end of rnd, k1f&b, k1—64 sts. Knit 10 rnds even, then rep inc rnd—68 sts. Knit 7 rnds—piece measures about 9¼" (23.5 cm) from CO.

*Handle:* *K11, BO 12 sts, k11, sl m; rep from * once more. *Next rnd:* *K11, use the backward loop method (see Techniques, page 113) to CO 12 sts, k11, sl m; rep from * once more. Knit 2 rnds even—piece measures about 10¾" (27.5 cm) from CO. BO all sts.

### Finishing

Weave in loose ends. Flatten bag so handles are centered on each side. With yarn threaded on a tapestry needle, sew across CO edge to close bottom of bag.

*Gussets:* Turn bag inside out, lay flat, and with yarn threaded on a tapestry needle, sew a short diagonal seam about 1" (2.5 cm) in from each corner (see Techniques, page 119) to shape lower corners of bag.

*Felting:* Felt according to instructions on page 116. Let bag air-dry thoroughly.

*Embellishing:* (optional) Sew 9 buttons to each side of bag, centered under the handle openings.

# SPIRAL
# RIB**bag**

I love the Bauhaus concept that form follows function. Putting this concept to work can be as easy as letting a stitch pattern dictate the design of a project, as in these drawstring bags. I began with a spiral rib pattern that curls around the bag body, then I bound off just the purl stitches in the rib pattern and continued working the knit stitches to form tassel-like tabs at the top. An I-cord drawstring threaded through eyelets makes the closure.

## SPIRAL RIB BAG

### Stitch Guide

*Spiral Rib Pattern* (multiple of 10 sts)

*Rnds 1 and 2:* *K5, p5; rep from * to end of rnd.

*Rnds 3 and 4:* K4, *p5, k5; rep from * to last st, end k1.

*Rnds 5 and 6:* K3, *p5, k5; rep from * to last 2 sts, end k2.

*Rnds 7 and 8:* K2, *p5, k5; rep from * to last 3 sts, end k3.

*Rnds 9 and 10:* K1, *p5, k5; rep from * to last st, end k4.

*Rnds 11 and 12:* *P5, k5; rep from * to end of rnd.

*Rnds 13 and 14:* P4, *k5, p5; rep from * to last 6 sts, k5, p1.

*Rnds 15 and 16:* P3, *k5, p5; rep from * to last 7 sts, k5, p2.

*Rnds 17 and 18:* P2, *k5, p5; rep from * to last 8 sts, k5, p3.

*Rnds 19 and 20:* P1, *k5, p5; rep from * to last 9 sts, end k5, p4.

Repeat Rnds 1–20 for pattern.

### Bag

*Sides:* With waste yarn, CO 50 (60) sts. Place marker (pm) and join for working in the rnd, being careful not to twist sts. With main yarn, work Rnds 1–20 of spiral rib patt (see Stitch Guide) once, then work Rnds 1–10 once more—piece measures about 5½" (14 cm) from CO.

*Tabs:* On the next rnd (Rnd 11 of patt), *BO 5 sts as if to purl, k5; rep from * to end of rnd—25 (30) sts rem; 5 (6) separate groups of 5 sts each. Working on the group of sts where yarn is attached, turn, and p5. If desired, place rem sts on holders. Cont on group of sts where yarn is attached as foll: (RS) K2, yo, k2tog, k1. Work 5 rows in St st, ending with a WS row. BO all sts as if to knit on next row. Return next group of 5 sts to needle and join yarn with WS facing. Complete as for first tab. Rep for rem groups of 5 sts—5 (6) tabs when all groups have been worked.

*Bottom:* Carefully remove waste yarn from provisional CO and divide 50 (60) live sts from base of CO as evenly as possible on 4 dpn. Place marker (pm) and join for working in the rnd. Work as foll:

*Rnd 1:* *Sl 1, k1, psso, k6 (8), k2tog; rep from * to end of rnd—40 (50) sts rem.

About 7 (8½)" (18 [21.5] cm) wide with bag laid flat, and 7 (8)" (18 [20.5] cm) tall from center of bottom to bind-off row for tabs.

### YARN
Chunky-weight (CYCA Bulky #5) yarn. *Shown here:* Colinette Chrysalis (94% cotton, 6% nylon; 91 yd [83 m]/100 g): #121 sunrise (pink multicolor) for small bag, and #55 toscana (green/yellow/rose/blue multicolor) for large bag.

### NEEDLES
Size 10 (6 mm): 16" (40 cm) circular (cir) and set of 5 double-pointed (dpn). Change needle size if necessary to obtain the correct gauge.

### NOTIONS
A few yards (m) waste yarn for provisional cast-on; stitch holders; tapestry needle.

### GAUGE
14 sts and 22 rows = 4" (10 cm) in spiral rib patt worked in the rnd.

*For smaller bag:*
*Rnd 8:* *K2tog; rep from * to end of rnd—5 sts rem. Proceed to Finishing.
*For larger bag:*
*Rnd 8:* *Sl 1, k1, psso, k2tog; rep from * to end of rnd—10 sts rem.
*Rnd 9:* Knit.
*Rnd 10:* *K2tog; rep from * to end of rnd—5 sts rem. Proceed to Finishing.

## Finishing

Break yarn, thread tail on a tapestry needle, gather through rem sts, pull tight, and fasten off. Weave in loose ends.
*Drawstring:* With dpn, CO 3 sts. Work 3-st I-cord as foll: *K3, with RS facing, slide sts to right needle tip and bring yarn around back of work in preparation to work another RS row; rep from * until piece measures 32 (36)" (81.5 [91.5] cm) from beg, or desired length. BO all sts. Thread drawstring through eyelets at top of bag.

*Rnds 2, 4, and 6:* Knit.
*Rnd 3:* *Sl 1, k1, psso, k4 (6), k2tog; rep from * to end of rnd—30 (40) sts rem.
*Rnd 5:* *Sl 1, k1, psso, k2 (4), k2tog; rep from * to end of rnd—20 (30) sts rem.
*Rnd 7:* *Sl 1, k1, psso, k0 (2), k2tog; rep from * to end of rnd—10 (20) sts rem. Cont as indicated for your size.

# GEOMETRIC ACCESSORY**bags**

*If you're like me, you can never have too many little bags to organize accessories, makeup, and small treasures. I used a variety of crochet stitches and geometric shapes for the three shown here. Each bag takes far less than a skein of yarn, so there's no reason you can't make all three. But be forewarned, the more you make, the more you'll want!*

## FINISHED SIZE

Square Bag: About 5" (12.5 cm) square
Rectangle Bag: About 7" (18 cm) wide and
5" (12.5 cm) tall.
Circle Bag: About 5¾" (14.5 cm) diameter.

## YARN

Worsted-weight (CYCA Medium #4) yarn.
*Shown here:* Square Bag: Louet MerLin
Camelot (70% worsted-spun merino wool,
30% wet-spun linen; 156 yd [143 m]/100 g):
#85 sunflower.
Rectangle Bag: Louet MerLin Avalon (70%
worsted-spun merino wool, 30% wet-spun
linen; 156 yd [143 m]/100 g): #55 willow.
Circle Bag: Louet MerLin Avalon (70%
worsted-spun merino wool, 30% wet-spun
linen; 156 yd [143 m]/100 g): #47
terra-cotta.

## HOOK

Square Bag: sizes F/5 (3.75 mm) and H/8
(5 mm).
Rectangle Bag and Circle Bag: size F/5
(3.75 mm). Change hook size if necessary
to obtain the correct gauge.

## NOTIONS

Tapestry needle; 7" (18 cm) zipper for
rectangle and circle bag; sewing needle
and matching thread.

## GAUGE

Square Bag: 18 sc and 22 rows = 4" (10 cm)
in single crochet with smaller hook.
Rectangle Bag: 24 sc and 22 rows = 4" (10 cm)
in single crochet; 15½ sts and rows = 4"
(10 cm) in pattern stitch.
Circle Bag: 24 sc and 22 rows = 4" (10 cm).

## GEOMETRIC ACCESSORY BAGS

### Notes

See Techniques, page 114, for basic crochet instructions.

The square bag is worked in one piece in a long strip, beginning at the top edge of one side, working down around the bottom, and back up to the top edge of the other side.

### Square Bag

With smaller hook, ch 26. Turn and sc in 2nd ch from hook. Work 1 sc in each ch across—24 sc. *Ch 2, turn, dc in each sc to end of row. Rep this row once more. *Next row:* Ch 1, sc in each st to end of row. Rep the last row until piece measures 9½" (24 cm) from starting ch. *Next row:* Ch 2, dc in each st to end of row. Rep the last row once more. *Next row:* Ch 1, sc in each dc to end of row. Fasten off.

### Finishing

Fold piece in half with RS facing tog and fold line at bottom of bag. With yarn threaded on a tapestry needle, sew side seams. Weave in loose ends. *Drawstring:* With larger hook and 2 strands of yarn held tog, ch 34. Fasten off. Beg at right side seam, weave drawstring through first row of dc, threading under 2 dc, then over 2 dc all the way around to end at the same side where you began.
*Tassels:* Make 2 tassels (see Techniques, page 121). Attach one tassel to each end of drawstring.
*Flower:* With smaller hook, ch 33. Sc in 2nd chain from hook, sc to end of row. Fasten off. Coil flower piece into rosette shape as shown, and with yarn threaded on a tapestry needle, sew to bag at desired location.

### Rectangle Bobble Bag

*Sides* (make 2)
Ch 29. Sc in 2nd ch from hook, sc in each ch to end—27 sc. Ch 1, turn, and work in patt as foll:
*Row 1:* (RS) *(Yo, insert hook into st, yo, draw loop through, yo, draw through 2 loops) 5 times in the same st, yo draw through 6 loops, 1 sc into each of next 2 sc; rep from * to end of row, ch 1, turn.

## Finishing

Place the two sides tog with RS facing each other. With yarn threaded on a tapestry needle, sew tog along two short sides and one long side, leaving rem long side open at top for zipper. Weave in loose ends. With sewing needle and thread, sew zipper to opening (see Techniques, page 121).

## Circle Bag

*Circle* (make 2)

Ch 5, sl st to first ch to join into a ring.

*Rnd 1:* Ch 1, work 10 sc into ring.

*Rnd 2:* Work 2 sc in each sc—20 sc.

*Rnds 3, 5, 7, 9, and 10:* Work 1 sc in each sc.

*Rnd 4:* *Work 1 sc in next sc, work 2 sc in next sc; rep from * around—30 sc.

*Rnd 6:* Rep Rnd 4—45 sc.

*Rnd 8:* *Work 1 sc in next sc, work 2 sc in next sc; rep from * to last sc, work 1 sc in last sc—67 sc.

*Rnd 11:* *Work 1 sc in next 2 sc, work 2 sc in next sc; rep from * to last sc, work 1 sc in last sc—89 sc.

Work 5 rnds even sc. Fasten off.

## Finishing

Weave in loose ends. Block to measurements. Place circles tog with RS facing each other. With yarn threaded on a tapestry needle, sew circles tog, leaving a 7" (18-cm) opening for zipper as shown. With sewing needle and thread, sew zipper to opening (see Techniques, page 121).

*Row 2:* Sc in each st to end of row, ch 1, turn—27 sc.

*Row 3:* *Sc in each of next 2 sc, (yo, insert hook into st, yo, draw loop through, yo, draw through 2 loops) 5 times in the same st, yo, draw through 6 loops on hook; rep from * to end of row, ch 1, turn.

*Row 4:* Rep Row 2.

Repeat Rows 1–4 four more times (20 patt rows total) or until piece measures 5" (12.5 cm) from beg, ending with a WS row. Work 1 more row sc. Fasten off. Push each bobble through to RS of fabric so all bumps are on the same side of piece.

# PETAL bib

*Sweeten up baby's mealtime, at least until the creamed spinach starts to fly, with this pretty petal bib. It's shaped with short-rows and fastens with an I-cord tie. And most important—it's machine washable, so cleanup's a breeze.*

## FINISHED SIZE
About 10" (25.5 cm) wide and 5½" (14 cm) long.

## YARN
Sportweight (Fine #2) yarn.
*Shown here:* Rowan Handknit Cotton (100% cotton; 93 yd [85 m]/50 g): #203 fruit salad (pink), #307 Spanish red, and #309 celery.

## NEEDLES
Size 6 (4 mm): straight and set of 2 double-pointed (for I-cord). Change needle size if necessary to obtain the correct gauge.

## NOTIONS
Stitch holders; tapestry needle.

## GAUGE
24 sts and 31 rows = 4" (10 cm) in St st.

## PETAL BIB

### Small Petal (make 1)
With straight needles, CO 10 sts. Knit 1 row. Cont as foll:
*Rows 1 and 3:* (RS) Knit into front and back of st (k1f&b), knit to last st, k1f&b—2 sts inc'd; 14 sts after Row 3.
*Rows 2 and 4:* (WS) K2, purl to last 2 sts, k2.
*Row 5:* Knit.
*Rows 6:* K2, purl to last 2 sts, k2.
Place sts on holder.

### Large Petal (make 4)
With straight needles, CO 10 sts. Knit 1 row. Cont as foll:
*Rows 1 and 3:* (RS) K1f&b, knit to last st, k1f&b—2 sts inc'd; 14 sts after Row 3.
*Rows 2 and 4:* (WS) K2, purl to last 2 sts, k2.
*Rows 5 and 7:* Knit.
*Rows 6 and 8:* K2, purl to last 2 sts, k2.
Place sts on holder.

### Join Petals
Place all five petals on straight needle with small petal in the center and two large petals on each side of small petal—70 sts total. Rejoin yarn with RS facing and work as foll:
*Rows 1, 3, and 5:* (RS) Knit.
*Row 2:* (WS) K2, [p10, k4] 4 times, p10, k2.
*Row 4:* K2, [p10, k1, k2tog, k1] 4 times, p10, k2—66 sts rem.
*Row 6:* K2, p11, [k1, p12] 3 times, k1, p11, k2.
Cont in short-rows as foll:
*Short-row 1:* K41 on RS, wrap next st (see Techniques, page 120), turn, p16 on WS, wrap next st, turn—25 sts rem unworked at each end of needle. *Note:* On the foll rows, hide any wraps as you come to them.
*Short-row 2:* K19, wrap next st, turn, p22, wrap next st, turn—22 sts rem unworked at each end of needle.
*Short-row 3:* K25, wrap next st, turn, p28, wrap next st, turn—19 sts rem unworked at each end of needle.

*Short-row 4:* (RS) K6, p3tog, k10, p3tog, k8, wrap next st, turn, p28, turn—62 sts total; 17 sts rem unworked at each end of needle.

*Short-row 5:* K30, wrap next st, turn, p32, wrap next st, turn—15 sts rem unworked at each end of needle.

*Short-row 6:* K9, p3tog, k8, p3tog, k11, wrap next st, turn, p32, wrap next st, turn—58 sts total; 13 sts rem unworked at each end of needle.

*Short-row 7:* K34, wrap next st, turn, p36, wrap next st, turn—11 sts rem unworked at each end of needle.

*Short-row 8:* K1, p3tog, k8, p3tog, k6, p3tog, k8, p3tog, k3, wrap next st, turn, p32, wrap next st, turn—50 sts total; 9 sts rem unworked at each end of needle.

*Short-row 9:* K34, wrap next st, turn, p36, wrap next st, turn—7 sts rem unworked at each end of needle.

Cont as foll:

*Row 1:* (RS) [K4, p3tog, k6, p3tog] 2 times, k11 to end—42 sts rem.

*Row 2:* (WS) K2tog, p38, k2tog—40 sts rem; all rem wraps have been hidden.

*Row 3:* Ssk, knit to last 2 sts, k2tog—38 sts rem.

*Row 4:* P2tog, purl to last 2 sts, p2tog through back loop (p2tog tbl)—36 sts rem.

*Row 5:* Ssk, k5, p3tog, k4, p3tog, k2, p3tog, k4, p3tog, k5, k2tog—26 sts rem.

*Row 6:* P2tog, purl to last 2 sts, p2tog tbl—24 sts rem.

*Row 7:* Ssk, knit to last 2 sts, k2tog—22 sts rem.

*Row 8:* Purl.

Cut yarn, leaving a 4" (10-cm) tail. Leave sts on needle and set aside.

## Finishing

*I-cord tie:* With dpn CO 3 sts. Work 3-st I-cord as foll: *K3, with RS facing, slide sts to right needle tip and bring yarn around back of work in preparation to work another RS row; rep from * until piece measures about 11" (28 cm) from CO.

*Join I-cord to bib:* (RS) *K2 I-cord sts, slip last I-cord st to right-hand needle knitwise with yarn in back, k1 from bib (live sts left on needle), pass slipped I-cord st over—1 st joined from edge of bib. Bring yarn around behind the I-cord in preparation for working another RS row as usual. Rep from * until all bib sts have been joined. Cont working 3-st I-cord until piece measures 11" (28 cm) from edge of bib. Cut yarn, thread on tapestry needle, draw through rem 3 I-cord sts, and fasten off.

Weave in loose ends.

# BABY**bolero**

A single ball of organically grown cotton yarn knits into an adorable and comfortable bolero jacket for baby's grand entrance. The back features an optional eyelet motif that, according to Eastern folklore, brings luck and protection to the wearer, no matter his or her size.

## FINISHED SIZE

About 15" (38 cm) chest circumference, with fronts overlapped slightly. To fit a newborn, teddy bear, or doll.

## YARN

Worsted-weight (CYCA Medium #4) yarn.
*Shown here:* Blue Sky Alpacas Organic Cotton (100% organic cotton, 150 yd [137 m]/100 g): #81 sand.

## NEEDLES

Body and sleeves: size 8 (5 mm). Edging: size 9 (5.5 mm): 24" (60 cm) circular (cir). Change needle size if necessary to obtain the correct gauge.

## NOTIONS

A few yards (meters) waste yarn for provisional cast-on; stitch markers (m); stitch holder; tapestry needle.

## GAUGE

18 sts and 22 rows = 4" (10 cm) in St st using smaller needles.

# BABY BOLERO

## Stitch Guide

*Eyelet Motif* (worked over 7 sts)
*Row 1:* (RS) K1, k2tog, yo, k1, yo, k2tog, k1.
*Rows 2 and 4:* (WS) P7.
*Row 3:* K2tog, yo, k3, yo, k2tog.
*Row 5:* K2, yo, k3tog, yo, k2.

## Body

With waste yarn and smaller needles, CO 67 sts. Change to main yarn.
*Row 1:* (RS) Knit.
*Row 2:* Purl.
*Row 3:* K1, M1R (see Techniques, page 118), knit to last st, M1L (see Techniques, page 118), k1—2 sts inc'd.
Rep Rows 2 and 3 two more times—73 sts. Cont even in St st until piece measures 1½" (3.8 cm) from CO, ending with a WS row. Work fronts and back separately as foll:
*Right front:* (RS) K20 for right front, place rem 53 sts on holder to work later. Work even in St st on 20 right front sts only until piece measures 1" (2.5 cm) from dividing row, ending with a WS row.
*Shape neck:* (RS) Ssk, knit to end—1 st dec'd. Purl 1 row. Rep the last 2 rows 9 more times—10 sts rem; armhole measures about 4½" (11.5 cm). BO all sts.
*Back:* Return 33 sts for back to smaller needle, and rejoin yarn with RS facing, ready to work a RS row. If working optional eyelet motif, cont even in St st until piece measures 2½" (6.5 cm) from dividing row, ending with a WS row; if not working the motif, work even in St st until piece measures 4¼" (11 cm) from dividing row, ending with a WS row, and then skip to "Shape neck" below. Mark center 7 sts for eyelet motif placement—13 sts at each side of center 7 sts. Cont working 13 sts each side in St st, and at the same time, work Rows 1–5 of eyelet motif (see Stitch Guide) over center 7 sts. When eyelet motif has been completed, cont even in St st across all sts until piece measures 4¼" (11 cm) from dividing row, ending with a WS row.
*Shape neck:* (RS) K10, place center 13 sts onto holder, join new yarn and

knit to end—10 sts at each side. Working each side separately, purl 1 row—armhole measures about 4½" (11.5 cm). BO all sts.

*Left Front:* Return 20 left front sts to smaller needle, and rejoin yarn with RS facing, ready to work a RS row. Cont even in St st until piece measures 1" (2.5 cm) from dividing row, ending with a WS row.

*Shape neck:* (RS) Knit to last 2 sts, k2tog—1 st dec'd. Purl 1 row. Rep the last 2 rows 9 more times—10 sts rem; armhole measures about 4½" (11.5 cm). BO all sts.

## Sleeves (make 2)

With larger needle and main yarn, CO 32 sts. Work p2, k2 rib for 3 rows. Change to smaller needles, and work even in St st until piece measures 1½" (3.8 cm) from CO. Beg with the next RS row, inc 1 st each end of needle every 4th row 4 times—40 sts. Work even until piece measures 4¾" (12 cm) from CO. BO all sts.

## Finishing

With yarn threaded on a tapestry needle, sew shoulder seams. Sew sleeves into armholes. Sew sleeve seams.

*Edging:* Carefully remove waste yarn from provisional CO and place 67 live sts on smaller needle. With RS facing, join yarn to bottom of left front opening, ready to work a RS row. With larger needle, k67 sts from provisional CO, pick up and knit 38 sts along right front to shoulder seam, 21 sts across back neck, and 38 sts along left front to bottom of front opening—164 sts total. Pm and join for working in the rnd. Work k2, p2 rib for 2 rnds. BO all sts in rib.

Weave in loose ends. Block lightly.

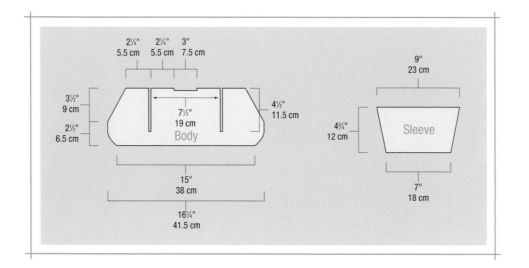

# BABY**hat**

*Few things are softer than a baby's skin, but the angora-blend yarn in this hat comes close. The hat is worked in the round from the scallop edging that frames baby's face to the gentle gathers at the top. Both sizes of hat can be made from the same skein of yarn, so you can knit one for now and one for baby to grow into.*

## BABY HAT

### FINISHED SIZE
About 13¾ (17)" (35 [43] cm) circumfer-ence. To fit newborn (12–18 months).

### YARN
DK or light worsted-weight (Light #3) yarn.
*Shown here:* Classic Elite Lush (50% angora, 50% wool; 123 yd [112 m]/50 g): #4460 autumn maroon (newborn) and #4433 wheat (12–18 months). One skein of this yarn will make both hats.

### NEEDLES
Size 7 (4.5 mm): set of 4 or 5 double-pointed (dpn). Change needle size if necessary to obtain the correct gauge.

### NOTIONS
Tapestry needle.

### GAUGE
21 sts and 28 rows = 4" (10 cm) in St st worked in the rnd.

### Stitch Guide
*Umbrella Pattern* (multiple of 18 sts)

*Rnd 1:* *K1, [k1, p3] 4 times, p1; rep from * to end of rnd.

*Rnd 2:* *K1, yo, k1, p2tog, p1, [k1, p3] 2 times, k1, p1, p2tog, k1, yo; rep from * to end of rnd.

*Rnd 3:* *K3, p2, [k1, p3] 2 times, k1, p2, k2; rep from * to end of rnd.

*Rnd 4:* *K2, yo, k1, p2, [k1, p1, p2tog] 2 times, k1, p2, k1, yo, k1; rep from * to end of rnd.

*Rnd 5:* *K3, [k1, p2] 4 times, k3; rep from * to end of rnd.

*Rnd 6:* *K3, yo, k1, p2tog, [k1, p2] 2 times, k1, p2tog, k1, yo, k2; rep from * to end of rnd.

*Rnd 7:* *K5, p1, [k1, p2] 2 times, k1, p1, k4; rep from * to end of rnd.

*Rnd 8:* *K4, yo, k1, p1, [k1, p2tog] 2 times, k1, p1, k1, yo, k3; rep from * to end of rnd.

*Rnd 9:* *K5, [k1, p1] 4 times, k5; rep from * to end of rnd.

*Rnd 10:* *K5, yo, ssk, [k1, p1] 2 times, k1, k2tog, yo, k4; rep from * to end of rnd.

*Rnd 11:* *K8, p1, k1, p1, k7; rep from * to end of rnd.

*Rnd 12:* Rep Rnd 11.

### Note
Be careful not to drop any yarnovers (yo) that happen to fall at the beginning or end of a needle.

## Hat

CO 72 (90) sts. Place marker (pm) and join for working in the rnd, being careful not to twist sts. Work Rnds 1–12 of umbrella patt (see Stitch Guide). Change to St st (knit all sts every rnd) and work even until piece measures 3¼ (4¾)" (8.5 [12] cm) from CO.

*Shape crown:* Dec as foll:

*Rnd 1:* *K7 (8), k2tog; rep from * to end of rnd—64 (81) sts rem.

*Rnd 2:* Knit.

*Rnd 3:* K6 (7), k2tog; rep from * to end of rnd—56 (72) sts rem.

*Rnd 4:* Knit.

Cont to dec every other rnd in this manner, working 1 less st between decs each dec rnd until you've worked a rnd of k4, k2tog—40 (45) sts rem. Dec every rnd, working 1 less st between decs until you've worked a rnd of k1, k2tog—16 (18) sts rem. *Next rnd:* *K2tog; rep from *—8 (9) sts rem. Break yarn, thread tail on a tapestry needle, draw through rem sts, pull tight, and secure to WS of hat. Weave in loose ends.

# 4 | make your house a home

# MOHAIR**pillows**

*These pillows will make great accents in any room in your home. Knit in two sizes and embellished with crochet motifs, buttons, and beads, they add color and texture to any setting. They are worked in the round, so the only seams to sew are at the top and bottom.*

## FINISHED SIZE
About 12 (14)" (30.5 [35.5] cm) square.

## YARN
DK or light worsted-weight (CYCA Light #3) yarn.
*Shown here:* Alchemy Promise (86% kid mohair, 14% nylon; 440 yd [402 m]/100 g): #042m silver. *Note:* 1 skein is needed for each pillow.

## NEEDLES
Size 6 (4 mm): 24" (60 cm) circular (cir). Change needle size if necessary to obtain the correct gauge.

## NOTIONS
Size I/9 (5.5 m) crochet hook; tapestry needle; 12 (14)" (30.5 [35.5] cm) knife-edge pillow form; 40 to 50 size 11 seed beads; assorted buttons measuring ⅛" (3 mm) to ¼" (6 mm); sewing needle and thread.

## GAUGE
22 sts and 25 rnds = 4" (10 cm) in St st; 26 sts and 25 rnds = 4" (10 cm) in k3, p3 rib.

## MOHAIR PILLOWS

### Note
See Techniques, page 114, for basic crochet instructions.

### Stitch Guide
*Flemish Motif*
With crochet hook and single strand of yarn, ch 8. Join with a sl st to form a ring.
*Rnd 1:* Ch 1, 16 sc into ring, sl st in first sc—16 sts.
*Rnd 2:* Ch 12 (counts as 1 tr and 8 ch), skip first 2 sc, [tr into next sc, ch 8, skip 1 sc] 7 times, sl st in 4th ch of ch-12.
*Rnd 3:* Ch 1, *into the next ch-8 arch work [sc, hdc, dc, 3 tr, ch 4, insert hook down through top of tr just made and work a sl st to close, 2 tr, dc, hdc, sc]; rep from * 7 more times, sl st in first sc in first arch. Fasten off.

*Acapulco Motif*
With crochet hook and 2 strands of yarn, ch 3. Join with a sl st to form a ring. Work in ring as foll:
*Rnd 1:* Ch 5 (counts as 1 dc and ch 2), [dc, ch 2] 7 times, sl st in 3rd ch of ch-5.
*Rnd 2:* Sl st in first space, dc in next dc, *[ch 5, sl st in 4th ch from hook] 2 times to make 2 picots, ch 1, dc in next space; rep from * a total of 7 times, [ch 5, sl st in 4th of these ch 5] 2 times to make 2 picots, ch 1, sl st in sl st at beg of rnd.
*Rnd 3:* *Sc between 2 picots, ch 7; rep from * 7 more times, sl st in first sc—8 ch-7 spaces.
*Rnd 4:* In each ch-7 space work [sc, 2 hdc, 4 dc, 2 hdc, sc], sl st in first sc. Fasten off.

### Pillow
CO 126 (157) sts. Place marker (pm) and join for working in the rnd, being careful not to twist sts. Place another marker after 63 (70) sts. Slipping markers every rnd, work as foll: K63 (70), work rem 63 (87) sts as [k3, p3] 10 (14) times, k3. Cont as established until piece measures 12 (14)" (30.5 [35.5] cm) from CO. BO all sts.

**Crochet motifs:** (shown on larger pillow) Make 1 Flemish motif and 1 Acapulco motif (see Stitch Guide). With sewing needle and thread, sew Flemish motif to lower right corner of pillow front. Secure each point of motif using sewing needle and thread as foll: Insert needle from WS to RS of pillow fabric, thread 1 seed bead on needle, insert needle back through fabric to WS in the same place to secure end of point with a single beaded stitch. Rep for rem points. Place Acapulco motif centered on top of Flemish motif, and tack lightly in place around the center of the motif, leaving petals free. If desired, add a cluster of 5 buttons of various sizes in the center, with 1 or 2 seed bead(s) on top of each button as shown.

**Seams:** Flatten pillow so the rib patt is centered on the back; the smaller pillow has a wider border of St st on each side of the rib patt, and the rib patt covers almost the full width of the back of the larger pillow. With yarn threaded on a tapestry needle, sew CO edge of pillow closed. Insert pillow form. Sew BO edge closed. Weave in loose ends.

## Finishing

Weave in loose ends.

**Buttons:** (shown on smaller pillow) With sewing needle and thread, attach buttons as desired, adding 1 or 2 seed bead(s) on top of each button as shown in photograph.

# BATH**mitt**
# AND**puffy**

*Refresh yourself while you bathe with an invigorating rub with a crocheted mitt or knitted puffy, both made from naturally abrasive aloo yarn imported from Nepal. The aloo plant is believed to have medicinal powers that can relieve headaches and fever. What better way to rejuvenate after a hard day? Like linen, the fibers have little elasticity and may be hard on your hands, but the toning rewards are worth the effort. Two seams transform a simple rectangle worked in Tunisian crochet into a practical bath mitt that fits over a hand or bar of soap. The puffy is knitted as a tube that is flattened, folded accordion style, then tied in the center with an I-cord rope.*

## FINISHED SIZE

Mitt: About 4½" (11.5 cm) wide and 6" (15 cm) long. Puffy: About 4" (10 cm) in diameter, after assembly.

## YARN

Worsted-weight (CYCA Medium #4) yarn. *Shown here:* Himalaya Yarn Aloo (100% nettle plant fiber; 150 yd [137 m]/100 g): #AL-00 natural. One skein is enough to make both projects.

## NEEDLES (FOR PUFFY)

Size 9 (5 mm): set of 4 or 5 double-pointed (dpn). Change needle size if necessary to obtain the correct gauge.

## HOOKS (FOR MITT)

Mitt: size N/15 (10 mm) afghan hook. Edging: size F/5 (3.75 mm) regular crochet hook. Change hook size if necessary to obtain the correct gauge

## NOTIONS

Tapestry needle; stitch marker for puffy.

## GAUGE

Mitt: 14 sts and 22 rows = 4" (10 cm) with yarn doubled in single Tunisian crochet with larger hook.
Puffy: 20 sts and 23 rows = 4" (10 cm) in St st, worked in the rnd.
Exact gauge is not critical for these projects.

## KNITTED PUFFY

CO 28 sts. Arrange sts as evenly as possible on 3 or 4 dpn, place marker (pm), and join for working in the rnd, being careful not to twist sts. Work even in St st (knit all sts every rnd) until piece measures 23½" (59.5 cm) from CO. *Note:* The fabric may bias slightly, but this will not affect the final product. BO all sts.

### Finishing

*I-Cord:* With yarn doubled, CO 3 sts. Work 3-st I-cord as foll: *K3, with RS facing, slide sts to right needle tip and bring yarn around back of work in preparation to work another RS row; rep from * until piece measures 19" (48.5 cm). BO all sts.

Weave in loose ends. Lay tube flat and fold into accordion pleats as shown below—folded bundle measures about 2½" (6.5 cm) wide and 3½" (9 cm) long. Wrap I-cord around center of tube, pull tight, and tie in a knot to secure. Tie ends of I-cord in an overhand knot to form a hanging loop. Fluff folds of tube into desired puffy shape.

## CROCHETED MITT

With yarn doubled and afghan hook, ch 16. Work Tunisian crochet (see Techniques, page 115), alternating one forward row and one reverse row, until piece measures 11¾" (30 cm) from beg. Fasten off.

### Finishing

Fold piece in half lengthwise with RS facing together; the fold line will be at the closed short end of the mitt. With yarn threaded on a tapestry needle, sew both side seams. Turn mitt right side out. *Edging:* Attach yarn to side seam at open end of mitt. With smaller crochet hook, work 2 sc in each st around opening; do not work sc into any of the seam allowance sts—about 60 sc around. Join with a sl st into first sc worked, ch 40 for hanging loop. Fasten off. Sew end of hanging loop to inside of mitt at side seam.
Weave in loose ends.

# BATH**mat**

*What could be better than stepping on this soft, cushiony mat after bathing? Thick and thirsty, the mat is crocheted in a simple lace pattern that uses single and double crochet. The yarn comes in one-pound cones in a wide range of colors, so you'll have no trouble matching any décor.*

## FINISHED SIZE

About 23" (58.5 cm) wide and 27"
(68.5 cm) long.

## YARN

Worsted-weight (CYCA Medium #4) yarn.
*Shown here:* Elmore-Pisgah Peaches &
Crème (100% cotton; about 840 yd
[768 m]/16 oz [454 g]): #3 cream
(pale yellow).

## HOOK

Size J/10 (6 mm). Change hook size if
necessary to obtain the correct gauge.

## NOTIONS

Tapestry needle.

## GAUGE

11 sts and 6 rows = 4" (10 cm) in pattern
st with yarn doubled.

## BATH MAT

### Mat

With 2 strands of yarn held tog, ch 65. Insert hook in 2nd ch from hook,
sc in each ch across—63 sc. Ch 2, turn, sc in each sc from previous row.
Ch 3, turn. Work patt st as foll:
*Set-up row:* Dc in first sc, ch 1, dc in next sc, [skip 1 sc, dc in next sc,
ch 1, dc in next sc] 20 times, dc in last sc—43 dc; 21 ch-1 spaces (sp).
Ch 3, turn.
*Pattern row:* (Dc, ch 1, dc) in each ch-1 sp across, dc in top of turning
ch at end of row—43 dc; 21 ch-1 sp. Ch 3, turn.
Rep the pattern row only until piece measures 26¼" (66.5 cm) from beg,
and ending last row by working ch 2, turn. *Next row:* Sc in each dc and
ch-1 sp across; do not work into turning ch at end of row—63 sc. Ch 2,
turn, sc in each sc from previous row. Fasten off.

### Finishing

Weave in loose ends. Block to measurements.

# FELTED **bowls**

I like colorful containers of every sort. Recently, I began making sturdy felted bowls and now have an assortment throughout my house. The bowls make colorful decorator accents and are ideal for organizing buttons, beads, yarn, keys, or other small objects that need a special place. I used a single color of yarn for each of the bowls shown here, but imagine the fun you can have with stripes!

## FINISHED SIZE

18 (22)" (45.5 [56] cm) circumference and
5½ (9¾)" (14 [25] cm) tall before felting;
17 (20½)" (43 [52] cm) circumference and
2½ (4½)" (6.5 [11.5] cm) tall after felting.
Measurements are approximate, with bowl
sitting flat on its base, and may vary slightly
depending on how the bowl is shaped during
the felting process.

## YARN

Chunky-weight (CYCA Bulky #5) yarn.
*Shown here:* Brown Sheep Lamb's Pride
Bulky (85% wool, 15% mohair; 125 yd
[114 m]/4 oz [114 g]): #113 oregano and
#185 aubergine for small bowls;
#102 orchid twist, #113 oregano, and
#185 aubergine for large bowls.

## NEEDLES

Size 15 (10 mm): 24" (60-cm) circular (cir)
and set of 4 or 5 double-pointed (dpn).
Change needle size if necessary to obtain the
correct gauge.
*Note:* While the pattern calls for both a 24"
(60 cm) circular needle and a set of dpns in
the same size, it can be awkward to work a
small number of stitches on the circular needle. The dpns can be used throughout to
resolve this issue.

## NOTIONS

Stitch markers (m); tapestry needle.

## GAUGE

10 sts and 13 rows = 4" (10 cm) in St st
worked in the rnd before felting. Exact gauge
is not critical for this project.

# FELTED BOWLS

## Bowl

CO 45 (55) sts. Place marker (pm) and join for working in the rnd, being careful not to twist sts. Work even in St st until piece measures 5½ (9¾)" (14 [25] cm) from CO.

*Shape bottom:* Dec as foll, changing to dpn when necessary:

*Rnd 1:* *Ssk, k5 (7), k2tog; rep from * to end of rnd—35 (45) sts rem.

*Rnds 2 and 4:* Knit.

*Rnd 3:* *Ssk, k3 (5), k2tog; rep from * to end of rnd—25 (35) sts rem.

*Rnd 5:* *Ssk, k1 (3), k2tog; rep from * to end of rnd—15 (25) sts rem. Cont as indicated for your size.

*For small bowl:*

*Rnd 6:* *Ssk, k2tog; rep from * to last 3 sts, ssk, k1—8 sts rem. Proceed to Finishing, below.

*For large bowl:*

*Rnd 6:* Knit.

*Rnd 7:* *Ssk, k1, k2tog; rep from * to end of rnd—15 sts rem.

*Rnd 8:* *Ssk, k2tog; rep from * to last 3 sts, ssk, k1—8 sts rem. Proceed to Finishing.

## Finishing

Break yarn, thread tail on a tapestry needle, gather through rem sts, pull tight, and fasten off. Weave in loose ends.

*Felting:* Felt according to instructions on page 116, and shape as desired.

# CANDY**wrapper**
# SACHETS

*To make a sachet that's almost too pretty to hide in a drawer or closet, knit up a decorative little tube, tuck some sweet-smelling lavender inside, and secure it in place with ribbon ties. I've provided a trio of stitch patterns, but feel free to experiment with your own designs. The sachets knit up quickly and use only a small amount of yarn, so before you know it, you'll have one for every drawer in the house. If you run out of drawers, add an extra length of ribbon to form a loop at one end and hang the sachets from hangers or hooks in your closet.*

## FINISHED SIZE

About 2" (5 cm) wide and 4" (10 cm) long, assembled and stuffed.

## YARN

Fingering-weight (CYCA Super Fine #1) yarn. *Shown here:* Jaeger Silk (100% silk; 203 yd [186 m]/50 g): #129 cosmos (pink) and #131 silver blue. *Note:* One skein of this yarn will make about 8 sachets.

## NEEDLES

Size 3 (3.25 mm): set of 4 or 5 double-pointed (dpn). Change needle size if necessary to obtain the correct gauge.

## NOTIONS

Tapestry needle; 5⅓ yd (4.9 m) of ⅜" (1-cm) ribbon, cut into 12" (30.5-cm) lengths; about 4 oz (114 g) of dried lavender (available where potpourri supplies are sold, or from natural food stores); 8 Japanese self-fillable tea bags (available at Japanese/Asian markets or online at www.inpursuitoftea.com); sewing needle and matching thread.

## GAUGE

30 sts and 36 rows = 4" (10 cm) in St st worked in the rnd.

# CANDY WRAPPER SACHETS

## Stitch Guide

*Embossed Stripes* (any number of sts)
*Rnds 1–4:* Knit.
*Rnd 5:* Purl.
*Rnds 6 and 7:* Knit.
*Rnds 8–19:* Rep Rnds 5–7 four more times.
*Rnd 20:* Purl.
*Rnds 21–24:* Knit.

*Diamonds* (multiple of 9 sts)
*Rnd 1:* K4, *p1, k8; rep from * to last 5 sts, p1, k4.
*Rnds 2 and 8:* K3, *p3, k6; rep from * to last 6 sts, p3, k3.
*Rnds 3 and 7:* K2, *p5, k4; rep from * to last 7 sts, p5, k2.
*Rnds 4 and 6:* K1, *p7, k2; rep from * to last 8 sts, p7, k1.
*Rnd 5:* Purl.
*Rnds 9–24:* Rep Rnds 1–8 two times.
*Rnd 25:* Rep Rnd 1.

## Notes

The silk yarn shown is fairly fragile and will sometimes leave a gap, or "ladder," as you change from one double-pointed needle to the next. To avoid ladders, work a few extra stitches onto each needle every now and then to shift the position of the spaces between the needles.

You may find it helpful to use 4" (10 cm) sock needles to make working in the round on a small number of stitches more manageable.

## Candy Wrapper Tube

CO 81 sts. Divide sts as evenly as possible on 3 or 4 dpn, place marker (pm) and join for knitting in the rnd, being careful not to twist sts.
*Beginning ruffle:*
*Rnd 1:* Knit.
*Rnd 2:* *K1, k2tog; rep from * to end of rnd—54 sts rem.
Rep Rnds 1 and 2 once more—36 sts rem.
*Eyelet rnd:* K2, *yo, k2tog, k4; rep from * to last 4 sts, yo, k2tog, k2.

*Body:* Work St st, embossed stripes, or diamonds (see Stitch Guide) as desired for 24 or 25 rnds. Rep eyelet rnd.

*End ruffle:* Cont as foll:

*Rnd 1:* *K1, knit into front and back of st (k1f&b); rep from * to end of rnd—54 sts.

*Rnd 2:* Knit.

Rep Rnds 1 and 2 once more—81 sts. BO all sts.

## Finishing

With tapestry needle, weave in loose ends.

*Filling:* For each sachet, fill one empty tea bag with about 3 tablespoons (44 ml) of dried lavender. Fold top ⅜" (1 cm) of bag over, and use sewing needle and thread to whipstitch (see Techniques, page 120) bag closed.

*Assembly:* Place lavender-filled bags inside knitted tube. Thread one 12" (30.5-cm) piece of ribbon through eyelets at each end of tube and pull tight to gather. Wrap the ribbon around the sachet a second time, and tie ribbon in a knot or bow.

# 5 | rediscover your stash

# CUP**cakes**

*I was so inspired by the knitted cupcakes on the cover of the 2004 edition of the Anthropologie holiday catalog that I decided to design my own version. After sifting through my stash of smooth yarns for the "papers," novelty yarns for the "icing," and buttons for the decorations, I came up with an assortment of knitted confections that would do a pastry chef proud. Although each cupcake knits up quickly, be forewarned— they tend to multiply.*

## FINISHED SIZE
About 3" (7.5 cm) diameter at base, 4" (10 cm) diameter at top, and 3½" (9 cm) tall.

## YARN
Base: DK or light worsted-weight (CYCA Light #3) yarn.
Top: Chunky-weight (CYCA Bulky #5) yarn.
*Shown here*: See box at right.

## NEEDLES
Base: Size 5 (3.75 mm): set of 4 or 5 double-pointed (dpn). Top (frosting): size 9 (5.5 mm): set of 4 or 5 dpn. Exact gauge is not critical for this project; select a needle size that will make a tight enough fabric to prevent stuffing from showing.

## NOTIONS
Tapestry needle; polyester fiberfill (4 oz [114 g] will stuff about 9 cupcakes); assorted buttons and/or seed beads for embellishments; sewing needle and thread.

## GAUGE
Depending on the yarn used, about 24–26 sts and 23–28 rows = 4" (10 cm) in k1, p1 rib using smaller needles.

## CUPCAKES

### Base
With smaller needles and light worsted or DK yarn, CO 56 sts. Divide sts as evenly as possible on 3 or 4 dpn, place marker (pm), and join for working in the rnd, being careful not to twist sts. Work in k1, p1 rib until piece measures 2¼" (5.5 cm) from CO. Purl 1 rnd.
*Shape base:* Cont as foll:
*Rnd 1:* *Sl 1, k1, psso, k4, k2tog; rep from * to end of rnd—42 sts rem.
*Rnds 2 and 3:* Knit.
*Rnd 4:* *Sl 1, k1, psso, k2, k2tog; rep from * to end of rnd—28 sts rem.
*Rnds 5 and 6:* Knit.
*Rnd 7:* *Sl 1, k1, psso, k2tog; rep from * to end of rnd—14 sts rem.
*Rnd 8:* *K2tog; rep from * to end of rnd—7 sts rem.
Cut yarn, leaving a 6" (15-cm) tail. Thread tail on a tapestry needle, draw through rem sts, pull tight, and fasten off to WS.

### Top
With larger needles and chunky yarn, CO 32 sts. Divide sts as evenly as possible on 3 or 4 dpn, place marker (pm), and join for working in the rnd, being careful not to twist sts. Work as foll:
*Rnds 1–3:* Knit.
*Rnd 4:* *K6, k2tog; rep from * to end of rnd—28 sts rem.
*Rnd 5:* *K4, k2tog; rep from * to last 4 sts, k4—24 sts rem.
*Rnd 6:* *K2, k2tog; rep from * to end of rnd—18 sts rem.
*Rnd 7:* *K2tog; rep from * to end of rnd—9 sts rem.
Cut yarn, leaving a 6" (15-cm) tail. Thread tail on a tapestry needle, draw through rem sts, pull tight, and fasten off to WS.

### Finishing
Add embroidery (see Techniques, page 116), beads, or buttons to top as desired. Weave in loose ends.
*Assembly:* Fill base with fiberfill to desired fullness. Place top over the base, covering the filling, and extending evenly beyond the base all the way around. With light worsted or DK yarn threaded on a tapestry needle, use a whipstitch (see Techniques, page 120) to sew base to top, being careful that the stitching does not show on the RS of the top.

*Here are the specifics for my cupcakes: Shown on page 86 from left to right:*

## Cupcake #1

*Base:* Rowan Wool Cotton (50% merino wool, 50% cotton; 123 yd [112 m]/50 g): #910 gypsy (deep wine).
*Top:* Adriafil Frou Frou (45% polyamide, 28% cotton, 27% acrylic; 82 yd [75 m]/50 g): #21 pink; Berroco Chinchilla (100% rayon; 77 yd [70 m]/50 g): #5344 pink champagne, 1 strand of each held together.

## Cupcake #2

*Base:* Lion Cotton (formerly Kitchen Cotton; 100% cotton; 236 yd [212 m]/5 oz [140 g]): #144 grape.
*Top:* Classic Elite La Gran Mohair (76.5% mohair, 17.5% wool, 6% nylon; 90 yd [82 m]/1½ oz [42 g]): #6501 white; Anny Blatt Nenuphar (100% polyamide; 59 yd [54 m]/ 50 g): #050 blanc (white), 1 strand of each held together.

## Cupcake #3

*Base:* Classic Elite Provence (100% cotton; 205 yd [187 m]/100 g): #2682 asparagus.
*Top:* GGH Esprit (100% nylon; 88 yd [80 m]/50 g): #06 white.
*Embellishment:* 14 buttons of various sizes in random placement.

## Cupcake #4

*Base:* Fiesta La Luz (100% silk; 210 yd [192 m]/2 oz [56 g]): #18 wild iris.
*Top:* Classic Elite Bravo (40% rayon, 35% mohair, 13% silk, 6% wool, 6% nylon; 48 yd [44 m]/50 g): #3701 mist (mixed light grays); GGH Soft-Kid (70% super kid mohair, 25% polyamid, 5% wool; 151 yd [138 m]/25 g): #1 (white), 1 strand of each held together.
*Embellishment:* Size 8 or 6 seed beads to match base color, sewn in loops of 3 beads at a time.

## Cupcake #5

*Base:* Rowan Handknit DK Cotton (100% cotton; 92 yd [84 m]/50 g): #203 fruit salad (pink).
*Top:* Same as for Cupcake #4.
*Embellishment:* Rowan Handknit DK Cotton #203 fruit salad for daisy stitches and triple-wrapped French knots.

*Shown on page 87 clockwise beginning at upper right:*

## Cupcake #6

*Base:* Fiesta La Luz (100% silk; 210 yd [192 m]/2 oz [56 g]): #15 pinon (green).
*Top:* Same as for Cupcake #1.

## Cupcake #7

*Base:* Louet Gems Opal (100% merino wool; 225 yd [206 m]/100 g): #50 sage.
*Top:* Same as for Cupcake #2.
*Embellishments:* Rowan Wool Cotton (50% merino wool, 50% cotton; 123 yd [112 m]/50 g): #957 lavish (deep rose) for triple-wrapped French knots.

## Cupcake #8

*Base:* Louet Gems Opal (100% merino wool; 225 yd [206 m]/100 g): #35 mustard.
*Top:* Same as for Cupcake #9.
*Embellishment:* 14 buttons of various sizes placed randomly.

## Cupcake #9

*Base:* Rowan Wool Cotton (50% merino wool, 50% cotton; 123 yd [112 m]/50 g): #943 flower (raspberry).
*Top:* GGH Esprit (100% nylon; 88 yd [80 m]/50 g): #06 white.
*Embellishment:* Louet Gems Opal (100% merino wool; 225 yd [206 m]/100 g): #35 mustard for daisy stitches and #50 sage for triple-wrapped French knots.

# POM-POM**boa**

*I feel adventurous when I wrap this boa around my neck. I want to set aside all things serious, get out, and have some fun. Maybe that's because it's such a treat to make all these pom-poms from different yarns. The boa is a great way to use up partial skeins left over from other projects—the more types of yarn, the better. To make the boa, simply string the pom-poms on a long crochet chain, leaving a little space between them so that the pom-poms on one end can hook around the cord on the other to serve as a fastening.*

## POM-POM BOA

### FINISHED SIZE
About 82" (208 cm) long.

### YARN
Assorted worsted-weight
(CYCA Medium #4) yarns.
*Shown here:* See box below.

### CROCHET HOOK
Size F/5 (3.75 mm) recommended; exact
hook size not critical for this project.

### NOTIONS
Tapestry needle; four pom-pom forms, one
each 2½", 3", 3½", and 4½" (6.5, 7.5, 9, and
11.5 cm) in diameter; scissors.

### Boa

*Chain:* With crochet hook, make a crochet chain (see Techniques, page 114) 82" (208 cm) long. Fasten off. Knot one end of chain to prevent pom-poms from sliding off as you string them.

*Pom-poms:* Make 25–35 pom-poms (see Techniques, page 118) in assorted sizes using assorted yarns.

### Finishing

With the unknotted end of crochet chain threaded on a tapestry needle, thread the center of each pom-pom onto the chain, leaving about ½" (1.3 cm) of space between pom-poms. Knot rem end of chain to secure pom-poms.

---

**Shown here:** Chain: Classic Elite Lush (50% angora, 50% wool; 123 yd [112 m]/50 g): #4460 autumn maroon.

Pom-poms: Adrienne Vittadini Fiora (44% mohair, 44% nylon, 6% wool, 6% polyester; 52 yd [48 m]/25 g): #10 cream.

Adriafil Frou Frou (45% polyamid, 28% cotton, 27% acrylic; 82 yd [75 m]/50 g): #22 ecru.

Alchemy Promise (86% kid mohair, 14% nylon; 440 yd [402 m]/100 g): #042m silver.

Blue Sky Alpacas Alpaca & Silk (50% alpaca, 50% silk; 146 yd [132 m]/50 g): #i10 ecru.

Cascade Pastaza (50% llama, 50% wool; 132 yd [120 m]/100 g): #064 dark gray.

Classic Elite Bravo (40% rayon, 35% mohair, 13% silk, 6% wool, 6% nylon; 48 yd [44 m]/50 g): #3701 mist (mixed light grays).

Classic Elite Lush (50% angora, 50% wool; 123 yd [112 m]/50 g): #4460 autumn maroon.

Fiesta Kokopelli (60% mohair, 40% wool; 130 yd [119 m]/4 oz): Russian olive.

GGH Taj Mahal (70% merino superfine wool, 22% silk, 8% cashmere; 93 yd [84 m]/25 g): #12 dark gray.

Habu Feather Moire (83% polyester, 17% nylon; 22 yd [20 m] ½ oz [14 g]): white.

Jaeger Chamonix (48% angora, 47% merino, 5% polyacrylic; 119 yd [109 m]/50 g): #900 limoges (dusty rose).

Le Fibre Nobili/Lane Cervinia Imperiale (80% superkid mohair, 20% nylon; 109 yd [100 m]/25 g): #4100 off-white.

Manos del Uruguay Wool (100% wool; 135 yd [123 m]/100 g): #026 rose.

Rowan Kidsilk Haze (70% super kid mohair, 30% silk; 229 yd [209 m]/ 25 g): #583 blushes (pink).

Rowan Polar (60% wool, 30% alpaca, 10% acrylic; 109 yd [100 m]/100 g): #642 lettuce.

Rowan Wool Cotton (50% merino wool, 50% cotton; 123 yd [112 m]/ 50 g): #943 flower (deep pink) and #957 lavish (dark plum).

# FELTED STRIPEDtote

*Stripes are a great way to use up partial skeins. You can make the stripes narrow or wide, you can include dozens of colors or just a few—the possibilities are endless. One of my favorite projects is to knit a striped wool bag, then felt it to soften the boundaries between the colors and produce a dense, long-wearing fabric. I used five colors in this bag—one for the base and four in a pattern of narrow stripes. Experiment with your stash to come up with other looks.*

## FINISHED SIZE

About 20½" (52 cm) wide at base, 23½" (59.5 cm) wide at top, and 23½" (59.5 cm) tall, before felting. About 11" (28 cm) wide at base, 13" (33 cm) wide at top, and 11¼" (28.5 cm) tall, after felting.

## YARN

Five colors of worsted-weight (CYCA Medium #4) yarn.
*Shown here:* Patons Classic Merino Wool (100% wool; 223 yd [204 m]/100 g): #231 chestnut brown, #238 paprika, #208 burgundy, #209 old rose, and #240 leaf green.

## NEEDLES

Size 10½ (6.5 mm): 24" (60 cm) circular (cir). Change needle size if necessary to obtain the correct gauge.

## NOTIONS

Stitch markers (m); tapestry needle.

## GAUGE

14½ sts and 21 rows = 4" (10 cm) in St st worked in the rnd before felting.

# FELTED STRIPED TOTE

## Stitch Guide

*Stripe Pattern* Work in St st as foll:
*Rows 1 and 2:* Leaf green.
*Rows 3 and 4:* Paprika.
*Rows 5–8:* Burgundy.
*Rows 9 and 10:* Old rose.
*Rows 11–14:* Burgundy.
*Rows 15 and 16:* Leaf green.
*Rows 17 and 18:* Paprika.
*Rows 19 and 20:* Burgundy.
*Rows 21–24:* Old rose.
Repeat Rows 1–24 for pattern.

## Tote

With chestnut brown, CO 150 sts. Place marker (pm) and join for working in the rnd, being careful not to twist sts. Work even in St st (knit every rnd) until piece measures 6½" (16.5 cm) from CO, placing another marker after the 75th st on the last rnd to indicate other side of bag. *Note:* Bag shaping cont at same time as stripe pattern is introduced; read the next section all the way through before proceeding. *Inc rnd:* K1, knit in front and back of next st (k1f&b), knit to 2 sts before next m, k1f&b, k1, slip marker (sl m), k1, k1f&b, knit to 2 sts before next m, k1f&b, k1—4 sts inc'd. Work 13 rnds even. Rep the last 14 rnds 4 more times—170 sts. *At the same time,* when piece measures 9½" (24 cm) from CO, knit 3 rnds with old rose, then work stripe patt (see Stitch Guide) until piece measures 21¼" (54 cm) from CO.
*Shape handles:* Cont in stripe patt, *k32, BO 21 sts, k32*, sl m; rep from * to * once more. *Next rnd:* Cont in stripe patt, *k32, use the backward loop method (see Techniques, page 113) to CO 21 sts, k32*, sl m; rep from * to * once more. Cont in stripe patt for 10 more rows—piece measures about 23½" (59.5 cm) from CO. BO all sts.

## Finishing

Weave in loose ends. Flatten bag so handles are centered on each side. With yarn threaded on a tapestry needle, sew across CO edge to close bottom of bag.

*Shape gussets:* Turn bag inside out, lay flat, and with yarn threaded on a tapestry needle, sew a short diagonal seam about 3" (7.5 cm) in from each corner (see Techniques, page 119) to shape lower corners of bag.

*Felting:* Felt according to the instructions on page 116. Fold the bag flat with a 2½" (6.5 cm) deep pleat at each side and allow to air-dry.

# KID'S COLOR BLOCK**cardigan**

*I love color and I love creating asymmetrical designs. The two come together in this unisex color-block cardigan sized for toddlers to ten-year-olds. In this version, I've used different colors of the same chunky yarn (one ball of each color), but it would also be fun to combine different yarn types—try fuzzy with smooth or variegated with solid.*

## FINISHED SIZE

About 24 (26, 28, 30, 32)" (61 [66, 71, 76, 81.5] cm) chest circumference. To fit sizes 2 (4, 6, 8, 10) years. Shown in sizes 24" (61 cm) here and on page 55; in size 30" (76 cm) on page 101.

## YARN

Chunky (CYCA Bulky #5) yarn.
*Shown here:* Louet Gems Sapphire (100% wool; 103 yd [94 m]/100 g): Size 24" (61 cm): #35 mustard, #47 terra-cotta, #02 tobacco, #39 fern green, and #55 willow. Size 30" (76 cm): #35 mustard, #39 fern green, #47 terra-cotta, #50 sage, #53 caribou, and #55 willow.

## NEEDLES

Size 10 (6 mm): straight and set of 4 or 5 double-pointed (dpn). Change needle size if necessary to obtain the correct gauge.

## NOTIONS

Tapestry needle; two ⅞ (⅞, ⅞, 1, 1)" (2.2 [2.2, 2.2, 2.5, 2.5]-cm) buttons; one snap; sewing needle and matching thread for attaching snap.

## GAUGE

15 sts and 22 rows = 4" (10 cm) in St st.

# KID'S COLOR-BLOCK CARDIGAN

## Stitch Guide

*Stripe Pattern* Work in St st as foll:
*Rows 1–4:* Beg with RS Row 1, work 4 rows fern green.
*Rows 5–8:* Work 4 rows willow.
Repeat Rows 1–8 for pattern.

## Notes

For sizes 24 (26, 28)", the back is worked in solid-color St st. For sizes (30, 32)" the back is worked in stripe pattern.

For sizes 24 (26, 28)", both sleeves are worked identically in stripe pattern. For sizes (30, 32)", the sleeves are worked in solid-color St st, using a different color for each sleeve.

## Back

With mustard (mustard, mustard, fern green, fern green) and straight needles, CO 45 (49, 52, 56, 60) sts. Beg with a RS row, knit 2 rows. Change to St st.
*For sizes 24 (26, 28)":* Work in St st until piece measures 11½ (12, 12½)" (29 [30.5, 31.5] cm) from CO. BO all sts.
*For sizes (30, 32)":* Work in stripe patt (see Stitch Guide), until 72 (76) stripe rows have been completed, ending with Row 8 (4) of patt—piece measures about (13¼, 14)" (33.5 [35.5] cm) from CO. BO all sts.

## Right Front

With terra-cotta (terra-cotta, terra-cotta, sage, sage) and straight needles, CO 32 (34, 35, 37, 39) sts. Beg with a RS row, knit 2 rows. Change to St st, and work even until piece measures 8 (8½, 8¾, 8¾, 9¼)" (20.5 [21.5, 22, 22, 23.5] cm) from CO, ending with a WS row.
*Shape neck:*
*Row 1:* (RS) [Ssk] 2 times, knit to end—2 sts dec'd.
*Row 2:* (WS) Purl to last 2 sts, p2tog through back loops (tbl)—1 st dec'd.
*Rows 3–8:* Rep Rows 1 and 2 three more times—20 (22, 23, 25, 27) sts rem after Row 8.

*Row 9:* (RS) Ssk, knit to end—1 st dec'd.

*Row 10:* (WS) Purl to last 2 sts, p2tog tbl—1 st dec'd.

*Rows 11–14:* Rep Rows 9 and 10 two more times—14 (16, 17, 19, 21) sts rem after Row 14.

*Row 15:* (RS) Ssk, knit to end—13 (15, 16, 18, 20) sts rem.

*Row 16:* (WS) Purl.

Rep the last 2 rows 0 (1, 1, 2, 3) more time(s)—13 (14, 15, 16, 17) sts rem. Work even in St st until piece measures 11½ (12, 12½, 13¼, 14)" (29 [30.5, 31.5, 33.5, 35.5] cm) from CO. BO all sts.

## Left Front

With tobacco (tobacco, tobacco, mustard, mustard) and straight needles, CO 32 (34, 35, 37, 39) sts. Beg with a RS row, knit 2 rows. Change to St st and work even until piece measures 6¾ (7, 7, 6¾, 7)" (17 [18, 18, 17, 18] cm) from CO, ending with a WS row.

*Shape neck:*

*Row 1:* (RS) Knit to last 4 sts, [k2tog] 2 times—2 sts dec'd.

*Row 2:* (WS) P2tog, purl to end—1 st dec'd.

*Rows 3–8:* Rep Rows 1 and 2 three more times—20 (22, 23, 25, 27) sts rem after Row 8.

*Row 9:* (RS) Knit to last 2 sts, k2tog—1 st dec'd.

*Row 10:* (WS) P2tog, purl to end—1 st dec'd.

*Rows 11–14:* Rep Rows 9 and 10 two more times—14 (16, 17, 19, 21) sts rem after Row 14.

*Row 15:* (RS) Knit to last 2 sts, k2tog—13 (15, 16, 18, 20) sts rem.

*Row 16:* (WS) Purl.

Rep the last 2 rows 0 (1, 1, 2, 3) more time(s)—13 (14, 15, 16, 17) sts rem. Work even in St st until piece measures 10¼ (10½, 10¾, 11¼, 11¾)" (26 [26.5, 27.5, 28.5, 30] cm) from CO, or 1¼ (1½, 1¾, 2, 2¼)" (3.2 [3.8, 4.5, 5, 5.5] cm) less than length of back and right front. BO all sts.

## Right Sleeve

With fern green (fern green, fern green, terra-cotta, terra-cotta) and straight needles, CO 24 (26, 26, 28, 30) sts. Beg with a RS row, knit 2 rows. Change to St st.

*For sizes 24 (26, 28)":* Work 4 rows in stripe patt—piece measures about 1" (2.5 cm) from CO.

*For sizes (30, 32)":* Work 4 rows in St st—piece measures about 1" (2.5 cm) from CO. Cont in stripe patt for sizes 24 (26, 28)", cont in solid-color St st for sizes (30, 32)", and *at the same time* inc 1 st each end of needle every RS row 5 (5, 5, 2, 2) times, then every 4th row 6 (4, 3, 2, 3) times, then every 6th row 0 (2, 4, 7, 7) times—46 (48, 50, 50, 54) sts. Cont even in stripe patt or solid color as established until piece measures 8¼ (9, 10½, 12, 12½)" (21 [23, 26.5, 30.5, 31.5] cm) from CO, ending with Row 4 or Row 8 of stripe patt for sizes 24 (26, 28)". BO all sts.

## Left Sleeve

With fern green (fern green, fern green, caribou, caribou) and straight needles, CO 24 (26, 26, 28, 30) sts. Work as for right sleeve (see Notes).

## Finishing

With yarn threaded on a tapestry needle, sew shoulder and side seams. Measure down 6 (6½, 6¾, 6¾, 7¼)" (15 [16.5, 17, 17, 18.5] cm) from shoulder seam along selvedges of back and fronts and mark with waste yarn. Sew top of sleeves between markers, matching the center of each sleeve with the shoulder seam. Sew sleeve and side seams.

*I-cord edging:* With fern green (fern green, fern green, caribou, caribou) and dpn, CO 3 sts. Work attached I-cord as foll: With RS facing and beg at right side seam, *k2, sl last I-cord st to right needle as if to knit, pick up

along the right front edge, turn the corner at beg of neck shaping, work I-cord around neck opening to beg of left front neck shaping, and turn corner once again.

**Buttonholes:** On the edge of left front opening, mark the position of two buttonholes 1" (2.5 cm) and 2½" (6.5 cm) down from top of neck edge. Work attached I-cord to first buttonhole position, then work 3 rows of I-cord without joining. Skip the next 2 or 3 rows of sweater edge to leave an unjoined gap for buttonhole, and resume working attached I-cord to next buttonhole position. *Tip:* Before working the second buttonhole, try passing a button through the first buttonhole to test the size. If necessary, rip back and fine-tune the buttonhole by working more or fewer rows of I-cord without joining, and skipping more or fewer rows of sweater edge before resuming attached I-cord. Work second buttonhole same as the first. Cont working attached I-cord down left front, turn corner at lower edge, and work to left side seam. Because left front is shorter than the back, work attached I-cord along back selvedge to corner, turn corner, and work across back to right side seam, ending at beg of I-cord. BO all sts. With yarn threaded on a tapestry needle, sew ends of I-cord tog.

Weave in loose ends. With sewing needle and thread, sew buttons in place opposite buttonholes. Sew one half of snap to RS of right front, in the corner at beg of neck shaping. Sew other half of snap to WS of left front to correspond to position of other half of snap.

and knit 1 st from sweater edge, pass slipped st over (1 st joined). With RS of I-cord still facing, slide sts back to tip of needle, ready to work another RS row. Bring yarn around in back of work; rep from *. Work attached I-cord in this manner along the lower edge of the right front to the front opening.

**Turn corner:** Work extra rows of I-cord without joining to turn the corner as foll: K3 I-cord sts (do not pick up st from sweater edge), slide sts back to tip of needle, work 1 row of attached I-cord, picking up 1 st in sweater corner, slide sts back to right needle tip, k3 I-cord sts (do not pick up st from sweater edge)—3 I-cord rows worked; 1 sweater st joined at corner. Cont to work attached I-cord

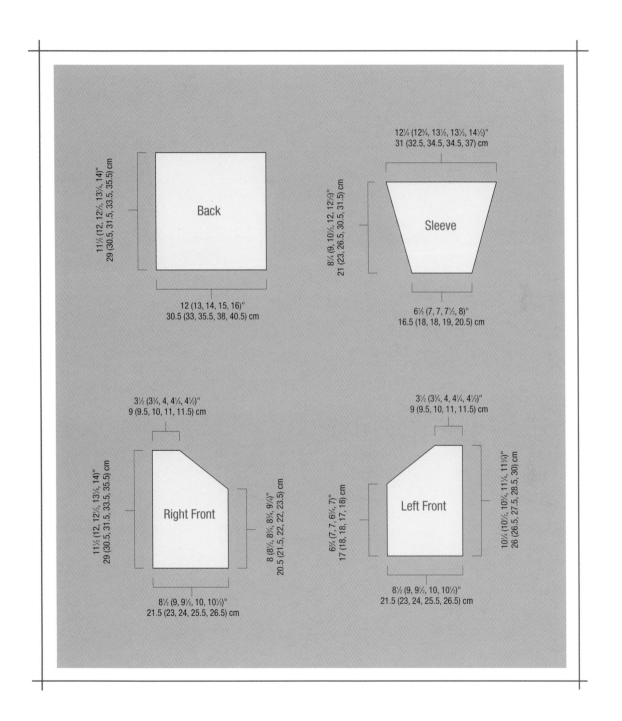

Back

11½ (12, 12½, 13¼, 14)"
29 (30.5, 31.5, 33.5, 35.5) cm

12 (13, 14, 15, 16)"
30.5 (33, 35.5, 38, 40.5) cm

12¼ (12¾, 13½, 13½, 14½)"
31 (32.5, 34.5, 34.5, 37) cm

Sleeve

8¼ (9, 10½, 12, 12½)"
21 (23, 26.5, 30.5, 31.5) cm

6½ (7, 7, 7½, 8)"
16.5 (18, 18, 19, 20.5) cm

3½ (3¾, 4, 4¼, 4½)"
9 (9.5, 10, 11, 11.5) cm

Right Front

11½ (12, 12½, 13¾, 14)"
29 (30.5, 31.5, 33.5, 35.5) cm

8 (8¼, 8¾, 8¾, 9¼)"
20.5 (21.5, 22, 22, 23.5) cm

8½ (9, 9½, 10, 10½)"
21.5 (23, 24, 25.5, 26.5) cm

3½ (3¾, 4, 4¼, 4½)"
9 (9.5, 10, 11, 11.5) cm

Left Front

6¾ (7, 7, 6¾, 7)"
17 (18, 18, 17, 18) cm

10¼ (10½, 10¾, 11¼, 11¾)"
26 (26.5, 27.5, 28.5, 30) cm

8½ (9, 9½, 10, 10½)"
21.5 (23, 24, 25.5, 26.5) cm

# STASH
# handbag

I like to experiment with different types of yarn, playing with arrangements to create fresh and unusual combinations. That's how I came up with the eclectic mix for this handbag, which I modeled after the shape of my favorite fabric purse. I used five different yarns, but you can use more or less, depending on what you have on hand.

## FINISHED SIZE

About 12" (30.5 cm) wide and 8" (20.5 cm) tall.

## YARN

Assorted chunky-weight (CYCA Bulky #5) and DK or light worsted-weight (Light #3) yarns.

*Shown here:*

Bag: Trendsetter Zucca (58% tactel, 42% polyamid; 72 yd [66 m]/50 g): #709 mauve; and Great Adirondack Waterfall (39% mohair, 7% wool, 54% nylon; 200 yd [182 m]/100 g): peacock.

Top trim and handles: Colinette Zanziba (50% wool, 50% viscose; 98 yd [89 m]/100 g): #102 pierro (green/yellow mix); Adriafil Frou Frou (45% polyamid, 28% cotton, 27% acrylic; 82 yd [75 m]/50 g): #22 yellow; and Elsebeth Lavold Cotton Patiné (100% combed cotton; 121 yd [110 m]/50 g): #010 honey.

## NEEDLES

Size 13 (9 mm): 24" (60-cm) circular (cir), size 11 (8 mm): 16" (40-cm) cir, and size 9 (5.5 mm): set of 2 double-pointed (dpn). Change needle size if necessary to obtain the correct gauge.

## NOTIONS

Stitch markers (m); tapestry needle; removable markers or safety pins; 7" (18 cm) zipper; sewing needle and matching thread for attaching zipper.

## GAUGE

10 sts and 15 rows = 4" (10 cm) in St st worked in the rnd on size 13 (9 mm) needle with 1 strand each of Zucca and Waterfall held together.

# STASH HANDBAG

## Handbag

With size 13 (9 mm) needle and 1 strand each of Zucca and Waterfall held tog, CO 62 sts. Place marker (pm) and join for working in the rnd, being careful not to twist sts; rnd begins at side of bag. Work even in St st (knit every rnd) until piece measures 6" (15 cm) from CO, placing another marker after the 31st st on the last rnd to indicate other side of bag.

*Shape pleats:* *K3, [sl 3 sts onto dpn and hold in front of work, knit these 3 sts tog with the next 3 sts on needle] 2 times, k1, [sl 3 sts onto dpn and hold in back of work, knit these 3 sts tog with the next 3 sts on needle] 2 times, k3, sl m; rep from * once—38 sts rem.

*Top trim:* Change to size 11 (8 mm) needle and 1 strand each of Cotton Patiné, Frou Frou, and Zaniba held tog. Knit 5 rnds. Purl 1 rnd. BO all sts kwise.

*Handles:* Lay bag flat. Measure in about 2½" (6.5 cm) from each side along top edge, just below the purl rnd, and place markers for handle position. Turn bag over and mark handle positions on other side. With size 9 (5.5 mm) dpn and 2 strands of Cotton Patiné held tog, pick up and knit 3 sts at marked handle position. *K2, bring yarn to front, sl 1, turn. Rep this row until handle measures 21½" (54.5 cm) from pick-up row. BO all sts. Sew BO end of handle to rem marked position on same side of bag. Rep for handle on other side of bag.

## Finishing

Weave in loose ends. Flatten bag so handles are centered on each side. With yarn threaded on a tapestry needle, sew across CO edge to close bottom of bag. Following the instructions on page 121, use sewing needle and thread to sew zipper into top opening.

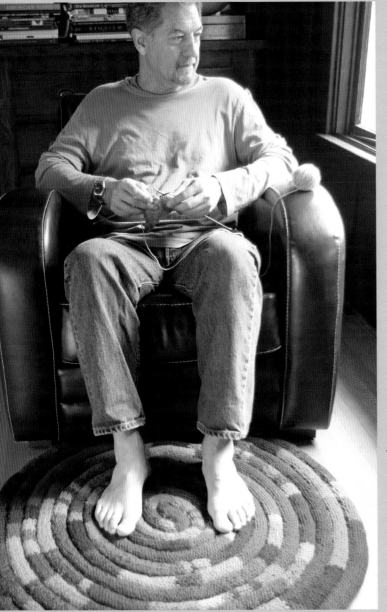

# LABYRINTH
# CIRCLE**rug**

*When I lived in San Francisco, I liked to walk the labyrinths at Grace Cathedral Episcopal Church. Intended to encourage reflection, the spiral walks—one inside, one outside—guide the traveler along a winding path that symbolizes the simultaneous changes and continuity of life. Knitting this rug is similar to one of those spiritual walks—the frequent changes in yarn and color provide an opportunity to pause and reflect on what you've done and to consider your next step—all as you maintain a continuous path.*

## LABYRINTH CIRCLE RUG

### Stitch Guide

*Slip Stitch Pattern* (multiple of 2 sts)
*Row 1:* *Sl 1, k1; rep from * to end of row.
*Row 2:* *Sl 1, p1; rep from * to end of row.
Repeat Rows 1 and 2 for pattern.

### Notes

Coil the knitting as it progresses to get an idea of how the colors will work together when the rug is assembled, and make any desired adjustments to the combinations.

Leave long enough tails for the stripes so you can sew the seam of the tube with yarn tails that match the color of each section.

### Rug

CO 20 sts. Following color sequence on pages 108 and 110 (read down each column), rep Rows 1 and 2 of slip st patt (see Stitch Guide) until piece measures about 19¾ yd (18 m). Cut yarn, leaving a 7" (18-cm) tail.

### FINISHED SIZE
About 33" (84 cm) diameter.

### NEEDLES
Size 11 (8 mm). Change needle size if necessary to obtain the correct gauge.

### YARN
Worsted-weight (CYCA Medium #4) yarn.
*Shown here:* See box below.

### NOTIONS
Tapestry needle; sewing needle; 20 yd (18.5 m) of ½" (1.3-cm) Wright's Piping Filler Cord (available at fabric stores); size .005 nylon transparent thread.

### GAUGE
About 18 to 20 sts = 4" (10 cm) in slip stitch pattern. Exact gauge is not critical, but fabric should be dense enough to completely cover cotton cording.

---

**Shown here:** Brown Sheep Lamb's Pride Worsted (85% wool, 15% mohair; 190 yd [174 m]/4 oz [114 g]): #47 Tahiti teal, #145 spice, #26 medieval red, #25 garnet, #113 oregano, #102 orchid, #175 bronze, #41 Turkish olive, and #29 Jack's plum. Cascade Pastaza (50% llama, 50% wool; 132 yd [121 m]/100 g): #64 gray.
Harrisville Designs New England Highland (100% wool; 200 yd [183 m]/100 g): #15 loden blue (teal), #19 blackberry, #7 tundra (yellow-olive), #36 garnet, #37 cocoa, #20 purple haze, #14 woodsmoke (light blue), #48 dove gray, and #68 olive.
Fiesta Kokopelli (60% mohair, 40% wool; 130 yd [119 m]/4 oz [114 g]): #12 roasted pinon.
Filtes-King Modigliani (100% merino wool; 71 yd [65 m]/50 g): #23 burgundy.
Louet Gems Sapphire (100% wool; 103 yd [94 m]/100 g): #58 burgundy and #39 fern green.

Manos del Uruguay (100% wool; 135 yd [126 m]/100 g): #G coffee, #M bing cherry, #68 citric (lime), #115 flame, #48 cherry, #59 kohl (charcoal), and #54 brick.
Mission Falls 1824 Wool (100% merino superwash; 85 yd [77 m]/50 g): #014 dijon and #030 teal.
Mountain Colors Weaver's Wool Quarters (100% worsted wool; 350 yd [320 m]/4 oz [114 g]): deep grape and granite peak.
Patons Classic Wool (100% merino; 223 yd [204 m]/100 g): #209 old rose, #219 ocean (blue), #240 leaf green, and #231 chestnut brown.
Reynolds Lite Lopi (100% wool; 109 yd [100 m]/50 g): #426 gold.
Rowan Rowanspun Aran (100% wool; 219 yd [200 m]/100 g): #972 hardy (green tweed).

Thread tail on tapestry needle, draw through sts on needle, pull tight, and fasten off.

## Finishing

Wrap knitted strip around ½" (1.3-cm) piping filler cord. With yarn tails threaded on a tapestry needle, sew edges of knitting closed around the entire length of the cording (see Notes), weaving in ends as you go. Before sewing seam for last stripe, trim cording to fit the tube, then close rem seam.

## Assembly

Coil covered tube into a circle, and use sewing needle and nylon transparent thread to firmly sew the coils together.

## Color Sequence (from center outward)

### Yarn Key

BSLP: Brown Sheep Lamb's Pride Worsted
CP: Cascade Pastaza
FM: Filtes-King Modigliani
HH: Harrisville Designs New England Highland
K: Fiesta Kokopelli
LGS: Louet Gems Sapphire
MDU: Manos del Uruguay
MFW: Mission Falls 1824 Wool
PCW: Patons Classic Wool
RLL: Reynolds Lite Lopi
RA: Rowanspun Aran
WW: Mountain Colors Weaver's Wool Quarters

| Knitted Length | Color | Knitted Length | Color |
|---|---|---|---|
| 2¼" (5.5 cm) | #47 Tahiti teal BSLP | ¾" (2 cm) | #113 oregano BSLP |
| 1½" (3.8 cm) | #145 spice BSLP | 7¼" (18.5 cm) | #25 garnet BSLP |
| 1" (2.5 cm) | #26 medieval red BSLP | 8" (20.5 cm) | #58 burgundy LGS |
| 2" (5 cm) | #64 gray CP | ¾" (2 cm) | #48 cherry MDU |
| 2¾" (7 cm) | #25 garnet BSLP | 2¼" (5.5 cm) | #G coffee MDU |
| 6" (15 cm) | #68 citric MDU | 2¼" (5.5 cm) | #23 burgundy FM |
| ½" (1.3 cm) | #113 oregano BSLP | 9¼" (23.5 cm) | #113 oregano BSLP |
| ½" (1.3 cm) | #68 citric MDU | 1½" (3.8 cm) | #36 garnet HH |
| ½" (1.3 cm) | #113 oregano BSLP | ½" (1.3 cm) | #59 kohl MDU |
| ½" (1.3 cm) | #68 citric MDU | 2" (5 cm) | #68 citric MDU |
| ½" (1.3 cm) | #113 oregano BSLP | ½" (1.3 cm) | #20 purple haze HH |
| 4¼" (11 cm) | #68 citric MDU | 7½" (19 cm) | #37 cocoa HH |
| 6¼" (16 cm) | #014 dijon MFW | 2" (5 cm) | #36 garnet HH |
| 11½" (29 cm) | #113 oregano BSLP | 2" (5 cm) | #972 hardy RA |
| 2" (5 cm) | #68 citric MDU | ¼" (6 mm) | #15 loden blue HH |
| 2¾" (7 cm) | #25 garnet BSLP | ¾" (2 cm) | #14 woodsmoke HH |
| 2½" (6.5 cm) | #G coffee MDU | 9½" (24 cm) | #59 kohl MDU |
| 2" (5 cm) | #15 loden blue HH | 2½" (6.5 cm) | #209 old rose PCW |
| 4½" (11.5 cm) | #19 blackberry HH | 2¾" (7 cm) | #19 blackberry HH |
| 1" (2.5 cm) | #7 tundra HH | 2½" (6.5 cm) | #68 citric MDU |
| 1½" (3.8 cm) | #36 garnet HH | ¾" (2 cm) | #219 ocean PCW |
| 1½" (3.8 cm) | #37 cocoa HH | ¾" (2 cm) | #15 loden blue HH |
| 10½" (26.5 cm) | #030 teal MFW | ¾" (2 cm) | #219 ocean PCW |
| 3" (7.5 cm) | #48 cherry MDU | 3¾" (9.5 cm) | #15 loden blue HH |
| 2½" (6.5 cm) | #7 tundra HH | ¾" (2 cm) | #48 cherry MDU |

| Knitted Length | Color |
|---|---|
| 1" (2.5 cm) | #54 brick MDU |
| 1" (2.5 cm) | #48 dove gray HH |
| 4" (10 cm) | #59 kohl MDU |
| 2½" (6.5 cm) | #36 garnet HH |
| 2" (5 cm) | #014 dijon MFW |
| 1¾" (4.5 cm) | #68 olive HH |
| 10" (25.5 cm) | #113 oregano BSLP |
| 4" (10 cm) | #102 orchid BSLP |
| 2" (5 cm) | #54 brick MDU |
| 5¾" (14.5 cm) | #240 leaf green PCW |
| 4" (10 cm) | #36 garnet HH |
| 4¾" (12 cm) | #37 cocoa HH |
| 1" (2.5 cm) | #48 dove gray HH |
| 2¾" (7 cm) | #19 blackberry HH |
| ¾" (2 cm) | #47 Tahiti teal BSLP |
| 1¾" (4.5 cm) | #14 woodsmoke HH |
| 4¼" (11 cm) | #39 fern green LGS |
| 3½" (9 cm) | #102 orchid BSLP |
| 1" (2.5 cm) | #19 blackberry HH |
| 16¼" (41.5 cm) | #47 Tahiti teal BSLP |
| 1" (2.5 cm) | #7 tundra HH |
| 2" (5 cm) | #20 purple haze HH |
| 1" (2.5 cm) | #68 olive HH |
| 2½" (6.5 cm) | #37 cocoa HH |
| 2¾" (7 cm) | #175 bronze BSLP |
| 2" (5 cm) | #54 brick MDU |
| 19½" (49.5 cm) | #25 garnet BSLP |
| 1½" (3.8 cm) | #59 kohl MDU |
| 1½" (3.8 cm) | #7 tundra HH |
| 1" (2.5 cm) | #25 garnet BSLP |
| 1" (2.5 cm) | #7 tundra HH |
| 1" (2.5 cm) | #25 garnet BSLP |
| 1" (2.5 cm) | #7 tundra HH |
| 1" (2.5 cm) | #25 garnet BSLP |
| 3¼" (8.5 cm) | #14 woodsmoke HH |
| 3¾" (9.5 cm) | #25 garnet BSLP |
| 1¾" (4.5 cm) | #175 bronze BSLP |
| 5" (12.5 cm) | #240 leaf green PCW |
| 21½" (54.5 cm) | #113 oregano BSLP |
| 2¾" (7 cm) | #20 purple haze HH |
| 1" (2.5 cm) | #19 blackberry HH |
| 1½" (3.8 cm) | #20 purple haze HH |
| ¾" (2 cm) | #19 blackberry HH |
| 1" (2.5 cm) | #20 purple haze HH |

| Knitted Length | Color |
|---|---|
| 2" (5 cm) | #7 tundra HH |
| 4" (10 cm) | #68 citric MDU |
| 6" (15 cm) | #113 oregano BSLP |
| 1" (2.5 cm) | #219 ocean PCW |
| 5¼" (13.5 cm) | #23 burgundy FM |
| 7½" (19 cm) | #102 orchid twist BSLP |
| 2½" (6.5 cm) | #26 medieval red BSLP |
| 4¼" (11 cm) | #G coffee MDU |
| 8¼" (21 cm) | #14 woodsmoke HH |
| 4" (10 cm) | #41 Turkish olive BSLP |
| 2½" (6.5 cm) | #7 tundra HH |
| 1¾" (4.5 cm) | #12 roasted pinon K |
| ½" (1.3 cm) | deep grape WW |
| ¾" (2 cm) | #12 roasted pinon K |
| ½" (1.3 cm) | deep grape WW |
| ¾" (2 cm) | #12 roasted pinon K |
| ½" (1.3 cm) | deep grape WW |
| 2½" (6.5 cm) | #47 Tahiti teal BSLP |
| 2" (5 cm) | #68 citric MDU |
| 2" (5 cm) | #115 flame MDU |
| 2" (5 cm) | #102 orchid BSLP |
| 7½" (19 cm) | #231 chestnut brown PCW |
| 2½" (6.5 cm) | #014 dijon MFW |
| 3¾" (9.5 cm) | #20 purple haze HH |
| 15" (38 cm) | #115 flame MDU |
| 3" (7.5 cm) | #36 garnet HH |
| 4¾" (12 cm) | #64 gray CP |
| 3¾" (9.5 cm) | #113 oregano BSLP |
| 2" (5 cm) | #219 ocean PCW |
| 1½" (3.8 cm) | #47 Tahiti teal BSLP |
| 1¾" (4.5 cm) | #240 leaf green PCW |
| 2" (5 cm) | #M bing cherry MDU |
| 1" (2.5 cm) | #26 medieval red BSLP |
| 27¾" (70.5 cm) | #25 garnet BSLP |
| 1½" (3.8 cm) | #426 gold RLL (2 strands held tog) |
| 6½" (16.5 cm) | #030 teal MFW |
| 18½" (47 cm) | #19 blackberry HH |
| 4" (10 cm) | #68 citric MDU |
| 11" (28 cm) | #47 Tahiti teal BSLP |
| 3¼" (8.5 cm) | #7 tundra HH |
| 5½" (14 cm) | #23 burgundy FM |
| 6¼" (16 cm) | #102 orchid BSLP |
| 1¾" (4.5 cm) | #145 spice BSLP |

| Knitted Length | Color |
|---|---|
| 5¼" (13.5 cm) | #G coffee MDU |
| 11½" (29 cm) | #030 teal MFW |
| 5" (12.5 cm) | #19 blackberry HH |
| 3" (7.5 cm) | #113 oregano BSLP |
| ¾" (2 cm) | #68 olive HH |
| 2" (5 cm) | #014 dijon MFW |
| 3" (7.5 cm) | #M bing cherry MDU |
| 9¼" (23.5 cm) | #26 medieval red BSLP |
| 8½" (21.5 cm) | #64 gray CP |
| 9¾" (25 cm) | #14 woodsmoke HH |
| 5¾" (14.5 cm) | #37 cocoa HH |
| 1½" (3.8 cm) | #19 blackberry HH |
| 11" (28 cm) | #41 Turkish olive BSLP |
| 1¼" (3.2 cm) | #219 ocean PCW |
| 1" (2.5 cm) | #48 dove gray HH |
| 1½" (3.8 cm) | #64 gray CP |
| 7" (18 cm) | #972 hardy RA |
| 2½" (6.5 cm) | #68 olive HH |
| 2½" (6.5 cm) | #23 burgundy FM |
| 4½" (11.5 cm) | granite peak WW |
| ½" (1.3 cm) | #29 Jack's plum BSLP |
| 12" (30.5 cm) | #G coffee MDU |
| 10½" (26.5 cm) | #20 purple haze HH |
| 1½" (3.8 cm) | #64 gray CP |
| ½" (1.3 cm) | deep grape WW |
| 5" (12.5 cm) | #14 woodsmoke HH |
| 5¾" (14.5 cm) | #47 Tahiti teal BSLP |
| 5½" (14 cm) | #41 Turkish olive BSLP |
| 3½" (9 cm) | #68 citric MDU |
| 4¼" (11 cm) | #41 Turkish olive BSLP |
| 6¾" (17 cm) | #23 burgundy FM |
| 2½" (6.5 cm) | #7 tundra HH |
| 1½" (3.8 cm) | #20 purple haze HH |
| 11" (28 cm) | #25 garnet BSLP |
| 4" (10 cm) | #G coffee MDU |
| 10½" (26.5 cm) | #29 Jack's plum BSLP |
| 1½ (1.3 cm) | #64 gray CP |
| 1" (2.5 cm) | #68 citric MDU |
| 11½" (29 cm) | #55 olive MDU |

*6* | glossary

# abbreviations

| | | | | |
|---|---|---|---|---|
| beg | beginning; begin; begins | | rnd(s) | round(s) |
| BO | bind off | | RS | right side |
| CC | contrast color | | sl | slip |
| cm | centimeter(s) | | sl st | slip st (slip 1 st pwise unless otherwise indicated) |
| cn | cable needle | | ssk | slip 2 sts kwise, one at a time, from the left needle to right needle, insert left needle tip through both front loops and knit together from this position (1 st decreased) |
| CO | cast on | | | |
| dec(s) | decrease(s); decreasing | | | |
| dpn | double-pointed needles | | | |
| g | gram(s) | | | |
| inc(s) | increase(s); increasing | | | |
| k | knit | | St st | stockinette stitch |
| k1f&b | knit into the front and back of same st | | tbl | through back loop |
| | | | tog | together |
| kwise | knitwise, as if to knit | | WS | wrong side |
| m | marker(s) | | wyb | with yarn in back |
| MC | main color | | wyf | with yarn in front |
| mm | millimeter(s) | | yd | yard(s) |
| M1 | make one (increase) | | yo | yarn over |
| p | purl | | * | repeat starting point |
| p1f&b | purl into front and back of same st | | * * | repeat all instructions between asterisks |
| patt(s) | pattern(s) | | ( ) | alternate measurements and/or instructions |
| psso | pass slipped st over | | | |
| pwise | purlwise, as if to purl | | [ ] | instructions worked as a group a specified number of times. |
| rem | remain(s); remaining | | | |
| rep | repeat(s) | | | |
| rev St st | reverse stockinette stitch | | | |

## BIND-OFFS

Figure 1          Figure 2

### Sewn Bind-Off

Cut yarn three times the width of the knitting to be bound off, and thread onto a tapestry needle. Working from right to left, *insert tapestry needle purl-wise (from right to left) through first two stitches (Figure 1) and pull yarn through. Bring tapestry needle knitwise (from left to right) through first stitch (Figure 2), pull yarn through, and slip this stitch off knitting needle. Repeat from *.

Figure 1          Figure 2          Figure 3

### Standard Bind-Off

Knit the first stitch, *knit the next stitch (2 stitches on right needle), insert left needle tip into first stitch on right needle (Figure 1) and lift this stitch up and over the second stitch (Figure 2) and off the needle (Figure 3). Repeat from * for the desired number of stitches.

## CAST-ONS

### Backward Loop Cast-On

*Loop working yarn counterclockwise and place this loop on the needle so that it doesn't unwind. Repeat from * for desired number of stitches.

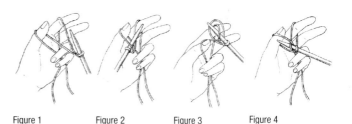

Figure 1      Figure 2      Figure 3      Figure 4

### Long-Tail (Continental) Cast-On

Leaving a long tail (about ½" to 1" [1.3 to 2.5 cm] for each stitch to be cast on), make a slipknot and place on right needle. Place thumb and index finger of left hand between yarn ends so that working yarn is around your index finger and tail end is around your thumb. Secure the yarn ends with your other fingers and hold palm upwards, making a V of yarn (Figure 1). *Bring needle up through loop on thumb (Figure 2), catch first strand around index finger with needle, and go back down through loop on thumb (Figure 3). Drop loop off thumb and, placing thumb back in V-configuration, tighten resulting stitch on needle (Figure 4). Repeat from * for desired number of stitches.

# CROCHET

## Crochet Chain (ch)

Make a slipknot and place on crochet hook. *Yarn over hook and draw the loop through the loop on the hook. Repeat from * for desired number of stitches. To fasten off, cut yarn and draw end through last loop formed.

Figure 1　　　　　　　Figure 2

## Double Crochet (dc)

*Yarn over hook, insert hook into a stitch, yarn over hook and draw a loop through (3 loops on hook), yarn over hook (Figure 1) and draw it through 2 loops, yarn over hook and draw it through the remaining 2 loops (Figure 2). Repeat from * for desired number of stitches.

Figure 1　　　　　　　Figure 2

## Half-Double Crochet (hdc)

*Yarn over hook, insert hook into a stitch, yarn over hook and draw a loop through stitch (3 loops on hook), yarn over hook (Figure 1) and draw it through all the loops on the hook (Figure 2). Repeat from * for desired number of stitches.

# CROCHET *continued*

Figure 1　　　　　　　Figure 2

## Single Crochet (sc)

*Insert crochet hook into stitch, yarn over hook and draw a loop through the stitch, yarn over hook (Figure 1), and draw loop through both loops on hook (Figure 2). Repeat from * for desired number of stitches.

## Slip Stitch Crochet (sl st)

Insert hook into stitch, yarn over hook and draw loop through stitch and loop on hook (Figure 1).

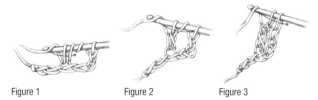

Figure 1　　　　Figure 2　　　　Figure 3

## Treble Crochet (tr)

*Wrap yarn around hook 2 times, insert hook into a stitch, yarn over hook and draw a loop through (4 loops on hook; Figure 1), yarn over hook and draw it through 2 loops (Figure 2), yarn over hook and draw it through the next 2 loops, yarn over hook and draw it through the remaining 2 loops (Figure 3). Repeat from * for desired number of stitches.

Figure 1

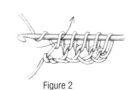

Figure 2

Figure 3

Figure 4

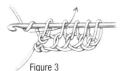

Figure 5

## Tunisian Crochet

*Foundation Row (pick up sts):* Insert afghan hook through top loop of second ch from hook (Figure 1), yarn over and draw through a loop (2 sts on hook). *Insert hook into top loop of next st and draw a loop through, leaving it on the hook. Rep from *, drawing 1 loop through each st, and leaving all loops on hook.
*Reverse Row (complete the st):* Yarn over hook and draw a loop through the first loop on hook (Figure 2) to create 1 turning ch and bring hook up to the level of the next row. *Yarn over and bring the hook through 2 sts (Figure 3). Rep from * to end of row, working from left to right and binding off 1 st each time you draw a

loop through 2 loops on hook, ending with 1 loop on hook (counts as the first st of the next row).
*Forward Row (pick up sts):* *Bring hook from right to left under the first vertical bar created by the first two rows (Figure 4) and draw a loop through (Figure 5), leaving it on the hook. Rep from * to end of row, drawing up a loop from under the last vertical strand. Work a Forward Row followed by a Reverse Row for pattern.

## DECREASES

### K2tog

Knit 2 stitches together as if they were a single stitch.

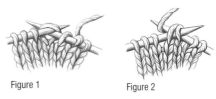

Figure 1

Figure 2

### Ssk

Slip 2 stitches individually knitwise (Figure 1), then insert left needle tip into front of these 2 slipped stitches, and use the right needle to knit them together through their back loops (Figure 2).

## EMBROIDERY

### French Knot

Bring threaded needle out of knitted background from back to front, wrap yarn around needle one to three times, then use your thumb to hold the wraps in place while pushing the needle through the wraps into the background a short distance from where it came out.

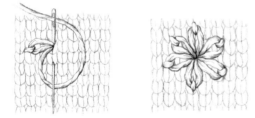

### Daisy Stitch

Bring threaded needle out of knitted background from back to front, *form a short loop and insert needle into background where it came out. Keeping the loop under the needle, bring the needle back out of the background a short distance away. Beginning each stitch at the same point in the background, repeat from * for the desired number of petals (six shown).

## FELTING

### Felting Guidelines

Fill washing machine with hot water at lowest water level possible and add 1–2 tablespoons of dishwashing soap. Place knitted piece in washing machine, along with a tennis shoe or some tennis balls for friction. Set machine to agitate and check progress every few minutes—felting time will vary, depending on temperature of water, type of soap, and intensity of agitation. When knitted stitches are no longer visible and the fabric is smooth and impermeable, remove the piece from the machine. Do not let the piece run through the spin cycle; doing so may cause permanent creases. Remove the piece, squeeze out the water, then roll it in a dry towel to remove excess water. Lay it flat to air-dry, checking on piece periodically and reshaping as needed. Depending on the climate where you live, it may take several days to fully dry.

## INCREASES

Figure 1          Figure 2

### Bar Increase (k1f&b)

Knit into a stitch but leave it on the left needle (Figure 1), then knit through the back loop of the same stitch (Figure 2) and slip original stitch off the needle.

### Raised Increase (M1)

If no direction is specified, work the left-slant increase.

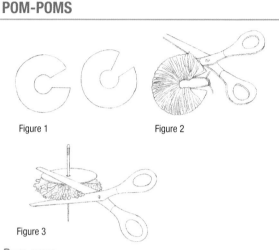

Figure 1          Figure 2

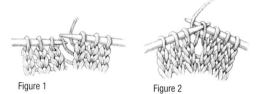

Figure 1                    Figure 2

*Left-Slant (M1L):* With left needle tip, lift the strand between last knitted stitch and first stitch on left needle from front to back (Figure 1), then knit the lifted loop through the back (Figure 2).

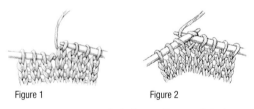

Figure 1                    Figure 2

*Right-Slant (M1R):* With left needle tip, lift the strand between last knitted stitch and first stitch on left needle from back to front (Figure 1), then knit the lifted loop through the front (Figure 2).

Figure 3

### Pom-pom

Cut two circles of cardboard, each ½" (1.3 m) larger than desired finished pom-pom width. Cut a small circle out of the center and a small wedge out of the side of each circle (Figure 1). Place a tie strand between the circles, hold circles together and wrap with yarn—the more wraps, the thicker the pom-pom. Insert scissors between circles and cut around outer edge to release the yarn. Knot the tie strand tightly (Figure 2). Fluff into shape and trim, if necessary. These instructions are reprinted with permission from *Nicky Epstein's Knitted Embellishments* (Interweave Press, 1999).

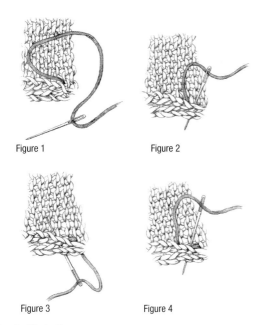

Figure 1

Figure 2

Figure 3

Figure 4

### Backstitch Seam

Working from right to left and 1/4" (6 mm) from the edge, bring threaded needle up through both panels of knitted fabric (Figure 1), then back down through both layers a short distance (about a row) to the right of the starting point (Figure 2). *Bring needle up through both layers a row-length to the left of the backstitch just made (Figure 3), then back down to the right, in the same hole used before (Figure 4). Repeat from *, working backward one row for every two rows worked forward.

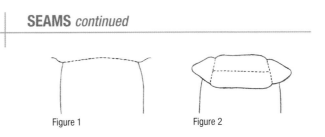

Figure 1

Figure 2

### Gusset Construction

With RS tog, sew CO edge closed (Figure 1). Flatten piece so that seam just worked is facing you and sew a short seam across each corner to form gussets (Figure 2).

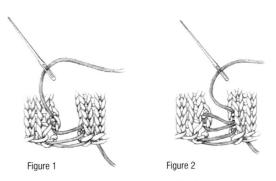

Figure 1

Figure 2

### Invisible Seam for Stockinette Stitch

Hold pieces to be seamed side by side, with their right sides facing upward. Thread seaming yarn on a tapestry needle and join the pieces as follows: *Insert threaded needle under horizontal bar at the base of the V of the first stitch on one piece (Figure 1), then under the bar at the base of the corresponding stitch on the other piece (Figure 2), pulling the seaming yarn firmly to bring the pieces together. Repeat from *, alternating a stitch from one piece and a stitch from the other piece.

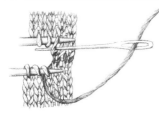

### Kitchener Stitch

Place stitches to be joined onto two separate needles. Hold the needles parallel with points facing to the right and so that wrong sides of knitting are facing each other.

*Step 1:* Bring threaded needle through front stitch as if to purl and leave stitch on needle.

*Step 2:* Bring threaded needle through back stitch as if to knit and leave stitch on needle.

*Step 3:* Bring threaded needle through the same front stitch as if to knit and slip this stitch off needle, bring threaded needle through next front stitch as if to purl and leave stitch on needle.

*Step 4:* Bring threaded needle through first back stitch as if to purl (as illustrated), slip that stitch off, bring needle through next back stitch as if to knit, leave this stitch on needle.

Repeat Steps 3 and 4 until no stitches remain on needles.

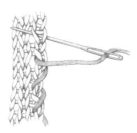

### Whipstitch Seam

Hold pieces to be seamed together so that their right sides face each other and so that the edges to be seamed are even with each other. Thread seaming yarn on a tapestry needle and join the pieces as follows: *Insert threaded needle through both layers from back to front, then bring threaded needle to back and repeat from *.

## SHORT ROWS

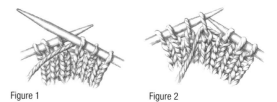

Figure 1          Figure 2

### Short-Rows

Work to the turn point (as specified in the instructions), slip the next stitch purlwise to the right needle. Bring the yarn to the front of the work (Figure 1), then slip the same stitch back to the left needle (Figure 2). Turn work and bring yarn between the needles and into position for next stitch, wrapping the slipped stitch as you do so.

*Hide the wraps on right-side (knit) rows as follows:* Work to just before the wrapped stitch, insert the right -

needle from the front, under the wrap from the bottom up, then into the wrapped stitch as usual. Knit them together, making sure that the new stitch comes out under the wrap.

*Hide the wraps on wrong-side (purl) rows as follows:* Work to just before the wrapped stitch, insert the right needle from the back, under the wrap from the bottom up, and place the wrap on the left needle. Purl the lifted wrap together with the wrapped stitch.

## TASSEL

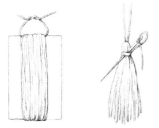

*Tassel*

Wrap yarn around a stiff form (cardboard works well) that is about 1" (2.5 cm) longer than desired finished tassel length—the more wraps, the thicker the tassel. Thread a 6" (15-cm) length of yarn under all wrapped strands at one edge of stiff form (Figure 1), pull tightly and knot securely. Cut yarn loops at the other edge. Cut a 12" (30.5-cm) length of yarn and wrap it tightly around loops a short distance from the topknot to form tassel neck. Knot securely, thread ends into tapestry needle and pull ends into center of tassel (Figure 2). Trim ends.

## ZIPPER

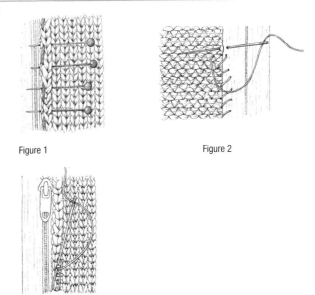

Figure 1                        Figure 2

Figure 3

*Zipper*

With right side of piece facing and zipper closed, pin zipper to fronts so front edges cover the zipper teeth. With contrasting sewing thread and right side facing, baste zipper in place close to teeth (Figure 1). Turn work over and with matching sewing thread and needle, stitch outer edges of zipper to wrong sides of knitted edge (Figure 2), being careful to follow a single column of stitches in the knitting to keep the zipper straight. Turn work so right side is facing, and with matching sewing thread, sew knitted fabric close to teeth (Figure 3). Remove basting stitches.

# bibliography

Budd, Ann *The Knitter's Handy Book of Patterns*
Interweave Press, 2002.

Carroll, Amy *The Pattern Library: Crochet*
Ballantine Books, 1981.

Drohojowska-Philp, Hunter *Full Bloom: The Art and Life of Georgia O'Keeffe*
Norton, 2004.

Epstein, Nicky *Nicky Epstein's Knitted Embellishments*
Interweave Press, 1999.

Galeskas, Beverly *Felted Knits*
Interweave Press, 2003.

Mon Tricot, *250 Patterns to Knit & Crochet*
Crown, (no date)

Stanley, Montse *Reader's Digest Knitter's Handbook*
Reader's Digest, 1993.

The Harmony Guides *220 Aran Stitches and Patterns Volume 5*
Trafalgar Square, 1998.

The Harmony Guides *300 Crochet Stitches Volume 6*
Collins and Brown, 2004.

Walker, Barbara *A Treasury of Knitting Patterns*
Schoolhouse Press, 2001.

# prop credits

page 34 Coat dress and crinolin
design by Claire LaFaye, available at Seaplane
www.e-seaplane.com or 503.234.2409

page 61 dress
design by Jamie Guinn
jamie@pdxapparelservices.com

# resources

## BEADS

### Dava Bead & Trade, Inc.
1815 NE Broadway Street
Portland, OR 97232
(877) 962-3282 for orders
www.davabeadandtrade.com

## BUTTONS

### Josephine's
521 SW 11th Avenue
Portland, OR 97205
(503) 224-4202
www.josephinesdrygoods.com

### The Button Emporium
914 SW 11th Avenue
Portland, OR 97205
(503) 228-6372
www.buttonemporium.com

## KNITTING NEEDLES

### Lantern Moon
(wholesale only; contact or check
website to locate a retailer near you)
(800) 530-4170
www.lanternmoon.com

## OTHER

### Labyrinth
Grace Cathedral Episcopal Church
1100 California Street
San Francsico, CA 94108
(415) 749-6300
www.gracecathedral.org/labyrinth

### Lavender
Purple Haze
www.purplehazelavender.com
Check the "Herb" listing in the phone
    book yellow pages for local sources.

### Japanese Tea Bags
Available at local Japanese/Asian
markets or online at inpursuitoftea.com
(item #XC530; package of 60 for $4).

## YARN COMPANIES

### Alchemy Yarns of Transformation
PO Box 1080
Sebastopol, CA 95473
(707) 823-3276
www.alchemyyarns.com

### Anny Blatt
7796 Boardwalk
Brighton, MI 48116
(248) 486-6160
www.annyblatt.com

### Berroco, Inc.
14 Elmdale Road
PO Box 367
Uxbridge, MA 01569
www.berroco.com

### Blue Sky Alpacas, Inc.
PO Box 387
St. Francis, MN 55070
(763) 753-5815
(888) 460-8862
www.blueskyalpacas.com

### Brown Sheep Company, Inc.
100662 County Road 16
Mitchell, NE 69357
(800) 826-9136
www.brownsheep.com

### Cascade Yarns
1224 Andover Park E.
Tukwila, WA 98188-3905
(800) 548-1048
www.cascadeyarns.com

### Classic Elite Yarns, Inc.
122 Western Avenue
Lowell, MA 01851
(978) 458-2837
www.classiceliteyarns.com

### Design Source (Manos del Uruguay)
38 Montvale Avenue, Suite 145
Stoneham, MA 02180
(781) 438-9631

### Elmore-Pisgah
204 Oak Street
Spindale, NC 28160
(828) 286-3665
www.elmore-pisgah.com

### Fiesta Yarns
5401 San Diego NE, Suite A
Albuquerque, NM 87113
(505) 892-5008
www.fiestayarns.com

### Great Adirondack Yarn Co.
950 County Highway 126
Amsterdam, NY 12010
(518) 843-3381

### Habu Textiles
135 West 29th Street, Suite 804
New York, NY 10001
(212) 239-3546
www.habutextiles.com

### Harrisville Designs
Center Village
PO Box 806
Harrisville, NH 03450
(603) 827-3333; (800) 338-9415
www.harrisville.com

**Himalaya Yarn, Inc.**
149 Mallard Drive
Colchester, VT 05446
(802) 862-6985
www.himalayayarn.com

**JCA, Inc. (Adrienne Vittadini; Reynolds)**
35 Scales Lane
Townsend, MA 01469

**Knitting Fever, Inc. (Araucania; Debbie Bliss; Elsebeth Lavold)**
PO Box 336
315 Bayview Avenue
Amityville, New York 11701
(516) 546-3600
www.knittingfever.com

**Koigu Wool Designs**
RR #1 Williamsford, ON
Canada N0H 2V0
(519) 794-3066
(888) 765-WOOL
www.koigu.com

**Lion Brand Yarn**
135 Kero Road
Carlstadt, NJ 07072
(800) 258-9276
www.lionbrand.com

**Lorna's Laces Yarns**
4229 N. Honore Street
Chicago, IL 60613
(773) 935-3803
www.lornaslaces.net

**Louet Sales (Gems; MerLin)**
808 Commerce Park Drive
Ogdensburg, NY 13669
(613) 925-4502
www.louet.com
*In Canada:*
RR 4 Prescott
ON Canada K0E 1T0

**Mountain Colors**
PO Box 156
Corvallis, MT 59828
(406) 961-1900
www.mountaincolors.com

**Muench Yarns & Buttons (GGH)**
1323 Scott Street
Petaluma, CA 94954-1135
(707) 763-9377
(800) 733-9276
www.muenchyarns.com

**Needful Yarns (Filtes King)**
60 Industrial Parkway
PMB #233
Cheektowaga, NY 14227
(866) 800-4700
www.needfulyarnsinc.com
*In Canada:*
4476 Chesswood Drive, Unit 10-11
Toronto ON M3J 2B9

**Patons Yarns**
320 Livingstone Avenue South
Listowel, ON
Canada N4W 3H3
(800) 265-2864
www.patonsyarns.com

**Plymouth Yarn Company, Inc. (Adriafil; Le Fibre Nobili)**
PO Box 28
Bristol, PA 19007
(215) 788-0459
www.plymouthyarn.com

**Trendsetter Yarns**
16745 Saticoy Street
Suite 101
Van Nuys, CA 91406
(818) 780-5497
www.trendsetteryarns.com

**Unique Kolours (Colinette; Mission Falls)**
28 N. Bacton Hill Road
Malvern, PA 19355
(800) 25-2DYE4
(610) 644-4885
www.uniquekolours.com

**Westminster Fibers, Inc. (Jaeger; Rowan)**
4 Townsend West, Unit 8
Nashua, NH 03063
(603) 886-5041
(800) 445-9276
for Rowan: www.knitrowan.com

# acknowledgments

No book is produced without the help of many talented people. I am especially grateful for the skillful expertise of my editor, Ann Budd; the multitalented Lori Gayle for her superb tech editing; and the staff at Interweave Press, most notably Linda Stark and Betsy Armstrong for providing me with the opportunity to photostyle and design my own book. Special thanks to Rebecca Campbell for keeping everything on schedule and for lending an ear, to Paulette Livers and Dean Howes for design production, and to Stephen Beal for careful copyediting.

Special thanks to John Mulligan whose beautiful photographs fill the pages of this book. And to models, Jameson Fisher, Lisa Jo Fisher, Teisha Helgerson, Matt Lounsbury, Henry Moreno, Avery Parker, Kate Towers, Morgan Whalen, and Sally Woodcock. Thanks also to Jennifer and Pied Cow Cafe, Krista and Fold Creperie, Lisa Jo Fisher, John Mulligan, and Karen Hite for welcoming us into their businesses and homes for photography.

Thanks to Jesse Stenberg and Lynn Gates who took knitting time away from their own work to knit (and crochet) several of the projects in this book.

Thanks to the following yarn companies: Anny Blatt, Berroco, Blue Sky Alpacas, Cascade Yarns, Classic Elite Yarns, Design Source, Fiesta Yarns, Great Adirondack, Harrisville Designs, JCA Inc., Knitting Fever Inc., Koigu Wool Designs, Mountain Colors, Muench Yarns and Buttons, Needful Yarns. Special thanks to Gina Wilde of Alchemy Yarns of Transformation and Beth Casey of Lorna's Laces Yarns for taking time to dye and prepare the colors I needed and to Brown Sheep Company, Habu Textiles, Himalaya Yarn, Lion Brand Yarn, Louet Sales, Unique Kolours and Westminster for providing yarn under sometimes tight deadlines.

Special thanks to Melissa Nelson Chakmakian and to the fabulous staff of Lint in Portland, Oregon, especially Emily Bixler, and Laura Irwin—your creativity, support, and feedback are irreplaceable! Thanks also to Morgan Whalen and Jo Mackby.

Friends and family make all things possible with their love and support. My brother Matt, whose continued encouragement and support keeps me reaching further and thinking more creatively. Thanks also to Dad, Carol, Elaine Chambers, Carol Leonard, Sue Stahl, and Dawn Witherspoon. Special thanks also to multi-talented photographer and friend Povy Kendal Atchison for making the process of creating my author photo such a pleasant experience and to friend Pam Gaier who took time away from a busy MBA schedule to help tweak and refine early drafts of my writing.

# index